THE TEMPLE

THE TEMPLE

A Book of Prayers

BY WILLIAM E. ORCHARD

Edited
and with a Foreword by
THE REVEREND
MARVIN HALVERSON

THE SEABURY PRESS · NEW YORK

Library of Congress Catalog Card Number: 65-22864

506-865-HC-4

Design by Nancy H. Dale

Printed in the United States of America

DEDICATED

to all those who, weary of fruitless quest and endless argument, are willing to try *the way of prayer*

❧ THE CALL

Come, my Way, my Truth, my Life:
Such a Way, as gives us breath:
Such a Truth, as ends all strife:
Such a Life, as killeth death.

Come, my Light, my Feast, my Strength:
Such a Light, as shows a feast:
Such a Feast, as mends in length:
Such a Strength, as makes his guest.

Come, my Joy, my Love, my Heart:
Such a Joy, as none can move:
Such a Love, as none can part:
Such a Heart, as joyes in love.

—from *The Temple,*
by George Herbert

◄§ FOREWORD
by the Reverend Marvin Halverson

THE PRAYERS in this collection were composed during Dr. William E. Orchard's unusual ministry at the King's Weigh House Church during the first quarter of this century. In itself, the setting of his ministry was uncommon. The King's Weigh House congregation went back to pre-Reformation times to a chapel founded by Queen Matilda and dedicated to St. Catherine. It was known as "peculiar" because it was not under episcopal jurisdiction and had the freedom of choosing its own priest. Located in East London, the original chapel building no longer stands.

At the passage of the Act of Conformity in 1662, the minister of St. Catherine's Chapel refused, like two thousand other clergymen of the Church in England, to subscribe. He and a portion of his congregation commenced in 1662 to hold services in a room above the King's Weigh House—the place where foreign goods were weighed for royal tax levy. The congregation grew, moved, and, after merging with the famous chapel of Dr. Thomas Binney, moved again to its present location just off Grosvenor Square in the West End of London.

There, the congregation erected a curious but assertive nineteenth-century version of a Gothic building.

The full glory of this church was manifested, however, in the ministry of William E. Orchard, who went there early in the twentieth century. Although he was a Congregational clergyman, his inclinations toward Anglo-Catholic and Roman Catholic practices in corporate worship prompted him to develop an order for Sunday morning worship which was nothing other than the celebration of the Eucharist in traditional eucharistic vestments, from which he changed to cassock and bands for preaching. Thus, Orchard sought in his ministry to conjoin what he understood to be catholic with a strong evangelical emphasis on preaching. His homiletical gifts were such that the Sunday evening services attracted throngs from all walks of life and ranks of society. It was in the setting of these evening services that Orchard offered the prayers included in this collection. They were truly common prayers in that they gathered up the doubt, the hunger, and the search of those who came to listen and try to pray.

It is not without interest that Dr. Orchard entitled this collection *The Temple,* for it calls to mind George Herbert's poems published with the same title. Of Herbert's *The Temple,* T. S. Eliot has observed:

> The content of the poems which
> make up *The Temple* . . . form a rec-
> ord of spiritual struggle which should
> touch the feeling and enlarge the un-
> derstanding of those readers also who
> hold no religious belief and find them-
> selves unmoved by religious emotion.*

In these respects, the poems of Herbert and
the prayers of Orchard bear a remarkable
similarity, a likeness which derives not simply
from their identical titles. Both men were
endowed with a deeply rooted faith, Orchard
entitling the autobiography of his spiritual
pilgrimage *From Faith to Faith*. Both were
devoted pastors, one to a simple Anglican
parish in the seventeenth century and the
other to a small Nonconformist London congregation, which was magnified by the throngs
that came to hear his preaching.

Herbert's poetry arose out of the tension
between his inherited faith and the new beliefs
of his century. Orchard's uncertainty and cre-
ativity arose out of the tension between evan-
gelicalism and catholicism. Both these laid
claim upon his mind and his heart. Late in
his life, he entered the Roman Catholic
Church. The prayers in *The Temple*, however,

* T. S. Eliot, "George Herbert" in *British Writers and
Their Work*, ed. by J. W. Robinson (Lincoln: Univer-
sity of Nebraska Press, 1964), pp. 67 and 69.

come out of that period in his life and ministry when the creative tension was at full tide
between these two poles of Christian faith and
life.

Throughout this collection, one catches over-
tones of the Church Militant, the Church
Universal, the Church Triumphant. But, pri-
marily, these are prayers of what Paul Tillich
has called the latent Church. So dissolved are
our ancient certainties, so broken is our common bond, and so feeble our faith, that truly
it might be said that these prayers of the
latent Church are the prayers of even the most
faithful among us today. They are prayers
which have the ring of sincerity and the note
of authenticity. They are prayers which have
become devotional classics for those who stand
on the threshold of belief. Thus, they both
speak to us and express on our behalf what
we try to utter to the Wholly Other.

ᕔᔒ PREFACE

SOME account of the origin of the prayers which compose this book may prove interesting to the reader and is perhaps necessary in order to prevent their improper use. Although they were mostly composed for use in congregational worship, the writer ventures to hope that they will not be used liturgically, and he does not recommend them as a model for public prayer. They were first of all written to serve the needs of a congregation which gathered on Sunday evenings to an ordinary Church Service, but which was composed very largely of those who had either lost faith in orthodox Christianity or were beginning to enquire their way into religion. The writer tried to put himself vicariously in the position of these people, and then to set his face Godward on their behalf. These prayers are gathered together mainly in the earlier part of the book, particularly in the sections called, "The Outer Gate," and "The Evening Sacrifice." The prayers in the later sections were mostly used at Morning Service, when the congregation was of a more confessedly definite Christian type.

It might also be explained that, although the prayers were written out carefully beforehand, they were not read in the Service, nor was any attempt made to commit them to memory. They were written out rather to prepare the writer's own mind and spirit. They were afterward corrected by the memory of their actual utterance and other ideas which found expression through the inspiration of the time were included. The intensely personal character of many of the prayers may surprise those who have made a study of what are called "Pulpit Prayers," but it ought to be stated that the Service in which they were used included liturgical prayers of the traditional type, which embraced more general needs. It is the conviction of the writer that public prayer ought to be either liturgical or personal, and that what is suitable for one type would be unsuitable for the other; every adequate service of prayer should contain both.

These prayers have now been gathered together to meet the needs of private devotion, in the hope that their somewhat unusual form may make them more attractive than books of prayer often are, and thereby the mere reading of them may set some unaccustomed feet upon the path of prayer. They are therefore recommended rather as meditative preparations for private prayer with the idea that they may stir the soul to adventure for itself upon this greatest of all unexplored territories. The plural form appropriate to common worship has been deliberately retained, in order to remind the novice that he does not set out upon this path alone, but in company with a great number, living and dead; and also as an acknowledgment that whatever inspiration these prayers may contain is derived from that mystical and interpenetration contact of souls which the effort to lead a congregation in prayer sometimes establishes.

The writer would offer these prayers as the best contribution he can make toward the solution, not only of the problem of prayer, but of the general problem of personal religion. One can argue about prayer and religion indefinitely, to very little effect; and although the writer is convinced that prayer is the highest exercise of the rational mind and religion is the very basis of all thought; yet it is impossible to give a full rational account of religion before one has awakened to the needs of one's own soul. And prayer is the very essence of religion; and the only way to solve the problem of prayer is by learning to pray.

To those who have yet to take the initial steps in the way of prayer, it may perhaps be permitted to make one or two recommendations; for it is the earnest hope of the writer that this book will find its way outside the circle of those who need no such instruction.

Preparation for prayer is almost more important than prayer itself. That preparation

ought to include some effort to compose the
mind by bringing it to silence. This need not
be of any great duration, but it ought to be
attained before one goes any further. Some
people find this very difficult to accomplish;
the modern mind can do anything but be still.
They are not helped by the advice of pseudo-
mysticism which recommends concentration
without providing anything on which to con-
centrate. But it offers what is sound enough
advice when it recommends certain devices
such as mental listening to the ticking of a
clock for a few seconds, or counting one's
breathing, though there is nothing mysterious
or mystic about such practices; they simply
suffice to engage the attention of certain areas
of mental activity and thus leave others free
for their higher functions.

Let there follow this first silence some fami-
liar ascription, such as: "Glory be to God on
high," or "Holy, Holy, Holy." If the spirit
takes fire at this let it have its way. If not, then
have ready to hand some prayers of the great
masters. Then let there be silence again to see
if the soul will stir on its own account; only
this time the silence needs to be longer. If
words now come, let them have free course,
and let the prayer be audible. This audible
prayer may pass into a still higher silence;
either the dumb stretching out toward God,
or the actual contemplation of His glory in

which every faculty is held awed and adoring. There is therefore a threefold silence possible in the upward movement of prayer. The silence which comes when the soul issues the command to every other faculty, "Be still"; the silence which may be described as "waiting on God," which is indeed the actual Hebrew for that expression; and the silence which God imposes, when there is with Him all the giving and with us nothing but the receiving. It must be understood, however, that this is an analysis of what happens rather than a prescription of what ought consciously to be followed.

Many will find that to have a special place set apart for prayer is a great help to devotion. It may be surrounded with everything that will keep the mind upon the object sought; and it will be found that in this direction catholic tradition has gathered up the richest and longest experience in the way of prayer. Others may fear or even despise outward aids; though they should be warned against any assumption that to do without them is a sign of superior grace.

Perhaps it is also necessary to remind the uninitiated that the setting apart of regular times of prayer, however short, is most desirable; and the value of them is not to be judged by the fact that these will rarely be the times of greatest devotion or when the heights of communion are attained; but they may be preparations for the great times. In the writer's very limited experience of these higher reaches of the life of prayer, he has always found that any great visitation of God, which has surprised the soul when it was not consciously seeking, has nevertheless nearly always followed some more assiduously disciplined season of prayer.

It needs to be said again that it is as a preparation entirely outside this process that these prayers are put forth. They are best described as "meditations"; but if they help anyone further along the way, even though it means casting this book aside as no longer of service, then the writer's purpose is served.

W. E. ORCHARD

❧ CONTENTS

✌ THE OUTER GATE

The good Lord pardon every one that setteth his whole heart to seek God, though he be not cleansed according to the purification of the sanctuary.

—*II Chronicles 30:18-19*

ETERNAL Father, Quest of ages, long sought, oft doubted or forsook; can it be that Thou art known to us, the Law within our minds, the Life of every breath we draw, the Love that yearneth in our hearts? Art Thou the Spirit who oft hast striven with us, and whom we greatly feared, lest yielding to His strong embrace we should become more than we dared to be?

An impulse toward forgiveness has sometimes stirred within us, we have felt moved to show mercy, the sacrificial life has touched our aspiration; but we were unprepared to pay the price. Was this Thyself, and have we turned from Thee? Something like this we must have done, so barren, joyless and so dead has life become. Canst Thou not visit us again?

We hush our thoughts to silence, we school our spirits in sincerity, and here we wait. O may we not feel once more the light upon our straining eyes, the tides of life rise again within our waiting hearts?

We never looked to meet Thee in the stress of thought, the toil of life, or in the call of duty; we only knew that somehow life had lost for us all meaning, dignity and beauty. How then shall we turn back again and see with eyes that fear has filmed? How can we be born again, now grown so old in fatal habit?

If we could see this life of ours lived out in Thee, its common days exalted, its circumstances made a throne, its bitterness, disappointment and failure all redeemed, then our hearts might stir again, and these trembling hands lay hold on life for evermore. Amen.

2 ₰

O GOD, Immortal and Invisible, forgive the faltering faith of those whose dwelling is among the mortal and the seen. We have no sight for unseen things, and we may have missed Thee at every turn. Every common bush may flame with fire, but we have no time to turn aside, and our hardened feet do not apprehend the holy ground. The heavens may declare Thy glory, but our eyes are too earthbound to read their story of infinity and peace. Day unto day may utter speech, but our ears are deaf with inward strife, and we hearken not nor understand. We have brooded long on the pain and anguish of the world, but we can read no redemption in the cross to which humanity is nailed; we have looked into the faces of our fellows, but discern no divine impression there; we have found little to love in the brother whom we have seen, how can we hope to love the God whom we have not seen? And now the awful fear has crept upon us that we are blind.

O Lord, that we might receive our sight.

Amen.

O THOU whom no man hath seen nor can see, the invisible cause of all that is visible, the reality beyond all appearance; how can we who are bound by sensuous things discern Thee?

The cares of the world, its insensate riches, its false standards have enslaved our souls, until the things that are seen have become our all.

Forgive us, O Unseen Spirit, if we have missed Thee and forgotten Thee. How shall we seek for Thee for whom our spirits yearn? For the things we see and feel only wake desires for something they are not. Shall we fast and pray, shall we separate ourselves from the world that is too much with us, shall we seek some quiet cloister of the soul?

Nay come to us, O Blessed, for we cannot come to Thee. Come to us in the life that entangles us, meet us in the common ways trodden by our busy feet, make Thy highways through the avenues of sense, clothe Thy glory in our failing flesh, breathe through the things that are seen the peace of the unseen and eternal. Amen.

4 &

O GOD, we turn to Thee in the faith that Thou dost understand and art very merciful. Some of us are not sure concerning Thee; not sure what Thou art; not sure that Thou art at all. Yet there is something at work behind our minds, in times of stillness we hear it, like a distant song; there is something in the sky at evening-time; something in the face of man. We feel that round our incompleteness flows Thy greatness, round our restlessness Thy rest. Yet this is not enough.

We want a heart to speak to, a heart that understands; a friend to whom we can turn, a breast on which we may lean. O that we could find Thee. Yet could we ever think these things unless Thou hadst inspired us, could we ever want these things unless Thou Thyself wert very near?

Some of us know full well; but we are sore afraid. We dare not yield ourselves to Thee, for we fear what that might mean. Our foolish freedom, our feeble pleasures, our fatal self-indulgence suffice to hold us back from Thee, though Thou art our very life, and we so sick and needing Thee. Our freedom has proved false, our pleasures have long since lost their zest, our sins, oh how we hate them.

Come and deliver us, for we have lost all hope in ourselves. Amen.

O FATHER, we turn to Thee because we are sore vexed with our own thoughts. Our minds plague us with questionings we cannot answer; we are driven to voyage on strange seas of thought alone. Dost Thou disturb our minds with endless questioning, yet keep the answers hidden in Thy heart, so that away from Thee we should always be perplexed, and by thoughts derived from Thee be ever drawn to Thee? Surely, our God, it must be so.

But still more bitter and humbling, O Father, is our experience of failure, so frequent, tragic and unpardonable. We have struggled on in vain, resolves are broken ere they pass our lips; we can see no hope of better things, we can never forgive ourselves; and after all our prayers our need remains and our sense of coming short but deepens. Yet, at least we know that we have failed, and how, if something higher than ourselves were not at work within?

Our desperate desires have driven us at last to Thee, conscious now, after all vain effort, that it is Thyself alone can satisfy, and now at peace to know that Thou it is who art desired, because Thou it is who dost desire within us. Beyond our need reveal Thyself, its cause and cure; in all desire teach us to discern Thy drawing near. Amen.

6 ℰ

O GOD, Holy above all thought, Holy past all vision, Holy beyond all bearing; how can we ask to look upon Thy face, how could we stand in Thy presence, how shall we abide the very thought of Thee? Yet none can escape Thee, none shut Thee out, none live apart from Thee. Only our blindness hides Thee from us, only our dullness passes Thee by, only our forgetfulness keeps Thee out of mind. Unheeding we climb the mount where Thy voice is uttered in thunder and Thy glance smites like lightning; none of us takes off his shoes, and none makes haste to veil his face. At the foot of a sorrowful cross we sit down to play; we heed no breaking heart, we feel no drops of blood, we lift our eyes only to mock and rail. We stand before the judgment seat, the books are opened, the truth shines clear, an awful hand divides us on the right and on the left; yet still we clasp our filthy rags about us, and make excuses to disguise our sins.

Dare we pray that our eyes should be opened? Should we not be overwhelmed with fear, smitten with sorrow, humbled to the breaking of our hearts?

Yet better far, O God, better far. Amen.

O GOD, who dwellest in light unapproachable and full of glory, why dwell we in darkness and in the shadow of death? The shadows of night which so quickly veil the glory of the day are not so heavy as those that rest upon our hearts. We are here for a moment, like a bird that flashes from the darkness, through the light, back to darkness once again. And even here as we pause awhile the shadows creep upon us. They rest upon those we love: they rest upon those into whose eyes we look: they rest upon ourselves. We cannot understand the brevity of life; we are just learning how to work, just catching some glimpse of its meaning; a sudden call, and we are gone. We cannot understand why such pain of body, heart, and mind, should sadden every day. We cannot understand why we should bring upon ourselves such misery, make such tragic failures of our life, or suffer such eternal loss.

Is it, O Father, that we see these shadows, because the Dayspring from on high hath visited us; that these pains are the feeling of those who wake from the stupor of death; that the darkness broods upon our hearts because we have turned our backs to Thee and hidden ourselves from Thy light?

Give us the grace, the daring, the desire to turn again that we may see Thy face. Amen.

8 ঽ

O GOD, who hast formed all hearts to love Thee, made all ways to lead to Thy face, created all desire to be unsatisfied save in Thee; with great compassion look upon us gathered here. Our presence is our prayer, our need the only plea we dare to claim, Thy purposes the one assurance we possess.

Some of us are very confused; we do not know why we were ever born, for what end we should live, which way we should take. But we are willing to be guided. Take our trembling hands in Thine, and lead us on.

Some of us are sore within. We long for love and friendship, but we care for no one and we feel that no one cares for us. We are misunderstood, we are lonely, we have been disappointed, we have lost faith in man and our faith in life. Wilt thou not let us love Thee who first loved us?

Some of us are vexed with passions that affright us; to yield to them would mean disaster, to restrain them is beyond our power, and nothing earth contains exhausts their vehemence or satisfies their fierce desire.

And so because there is no answer, no end or satisfaction in ourselves; and because we are what we are, and yet long to be so different; we believe Thou art, and that Thou dost understand us. By faith we feel after Thee, through love we find the way, in hope we bring ourselves to Thee. Amen.

O GOD, we have heard Thy call sounding in our ears; in youth and in age, in sickness and in health, in joy and in sorrow, at morning and at eventide; in the voice of nature, from the page of history, leaping from the lips of men, stirring in our own thoughts, crying from our poor desolate hearts. Yet we have not yielded ourselves to Thee.

We have been afraid lest we should lose something dear to us; our comfort, our content, our pleasure. Yet refusing we have lost our all, love and light and life itself.

We have been afraid lest we should lose ourselves in Thy being, lest the direction of our lives should be wrested from our hands, lest our wills should become as not our own. And now our wills are broken, we cannot direct our lives even where we would, and our very souls within are hard to find.

We have been afraid of the burden of Thy love. It seemed too hard to care for those we find it easier far to hate, to love those from whom our natures shrink, to break our heart over those who seem worthless, to spend our life for those who are hopeless. And now we are enslaved to self; we move among our fellows alien, afraid and lonely; we are weary of our carefulness and calculating ways.

O save us. Make us willing to be what we were meant to be. Give us the courage to forsake all and yield to Thee, ere it be too late.

Amen.

10 ౭◞

O FATHER, who hast set us amid the bonds of time; this hurrying pace of life frightens and amazes us. We cannot crowd our purposes into such a narrow space. Ere ever the day has worn to noon, or we have even planned the work we meant to do, the night comes down upon us and we can work no more. The swift years pass and find us little farther on. We wake to mourn what we have missed, to value most what comes no more.

Forgive our waste of precious moments, our loitering feet, our procrastinating will. O teach us to number our days, that we may apply our hearts to wisdom; to lengthen our brief life by intensity of living; to fill swift hours with mighty deeds; to lay up treasure where neither moth nor rust doth corrupt.

Seeing we spend our days as a tale that is told, let us haste to speak that which is within us, lest we be called away before the story is begun. If there is anything Thou hast meant us to do in life, O spare us till we have accomplished it. If there is any kindness we can shew, may we not neglect or defer it, seeing that we pass this way but once.

So may the very stress of earthly life educate us for the life eternal. Amen.

O THOU Desire of nations, by whom the prophets spake, of whom the poets dream, for whom the people long; when wilt Thou dawn upon our waiting vision? Age after age the heavens are scanned for the sign of Thine appearing. We watch for Thee more than they that watch for the morning. Yet all things continue as they have been from the beginning. Man labors still for wrong, sees the fruit of honest toil torn from him, and mingles tears with hopeless tasks. Still men sell their souls for a price and women are forced to a traffic of shame. The poor cry for bread and are offered a stone. Not yet do we see the mighty cast down from their seat; not yet hast Thou exalted the humble and meek; the race is still to the swift and the battle to the strong. Where is the promise of Thy coming?

Forgive the impatience, O our God, that would fling itself upon Thy slowly turning chariot wheels. Thou Thyself hast bid us watch and pray for the coming of Thy kingdom. The promise was it should be soon.

Perhaps Thou hast come, and the earth has rejected Thee; come like a thief in the night— and gone; come disguised as a child seeking love, a woman seeking justice, a man seeking souls, and we found no room for Thee. Then, O come back to us again.

Or dost Thou wait till we are ready? Dost

Thou tarry till we turn from the trifles that now hold our hearts? Must we ourselves prepare the way?

O help us to understand.

Amen.

12 ɜ❧

ALMIGHTY God, who sustainest man's spirit by an undying hope, hast taught us to look for a perfect revelation of Thyself, and bade us watch for Thy coming; be patient with our impatience when we cry in bitterness, How long? when in doubt and desolation we faint for a glimpse of Thy face. The heavens keep their dreadful order, the silence of the infinite spaces terrifies our minds; on earth tyranny, evil, poverty and sin retain their ancient power. Generations suffer, toil and pass away uncomforted and hopeless. The same veil of mystery hides the truth and all man's learning leaves him still unsure.

Are we in Thy presence and know it not; has the judgment commenced though we go about our careless ways? We fear a future hell, while already flames the quenchless fire, and the worm that dies not feeds upon our flesh. We look for a distant heaven, while it is all around us, if we care to walk its streets. The stones of the new Jerusalem lie ready to our hands, but we have rejected the chief corner stone.

Then let knowledge grow, the light dawn, and our eyes waken to reality. Or if we still must wait Thy time, then, though faith and love both die within the heart of man, let not hope depart, lest we sink in sight of port and lose our way with the city clear before us.

Amen.

13 ⤦

OUT of the depths have we cried unto Thee, O God; O God hear our prayer. Our desperate need of Thee is mocked by our faint and feeble petitions. Hearken not to the words of our lips disciplined by such fatal habit to conceal ourselves, but consider our travail of soul and listen to the groanings that cannot be uttered.

When we have dared to descend within, fathomless deeps make us afraid, and we dread to know ourselves; passions sleep within which any wandering breeze might stir to storm, and we be overwhelmed beneath its waves. Surely this cannot be ourselves, for of this we are afraid.

Deep within we have caught a glimpse of smiling seas which mirror the beauty of the sky, while they themselves are dark and foul; strange self-deceptions make us crave for comfort, while we sing of sacrifice; we pretend to love Thee, but love better still ambition, praise, the hollow word. If this should be ourselves, all hope for us is gone. Thou canst not love what we can only hate.

Yet, deeper still, O God, lies hunger for Thyself, and this must be of Thee, yet we fear this most of all. If this should pass our power to bear, we might be swept beyond our studied selfishness, our calculating prudence, and never be the same again.

Out of such depths we cry unto Thee, O God. Amen.

O GOD, Life Eternal, save us ere we die. Our days are speeding fast away, the things we meant to do are still undone, what we meant to be we feel we never shall be now, and night is nigh.

O leave us not.

Sometimes we fear that life itself is dying down within us, learning comes no longer easy to us, change makes us afraid, enthusiasm fades, resolve proves impotent.

O take not Thy Holy Spirit from us.

We have so carefully husbanded our resources, yet they have steadily declined. We have hoarded our powers, but what we kept we lost, only what we gave remained our own; and that is, oh so small. We have sheltered our souls from the chill of criticism, and daily have grown weaker; we have excused ourselves from arduous tasks, only to lose our rest; we have shrunk from pain, only to find the fear of life invade and terrify our hearts.

O cast us not away from Thy presence.

Amen.

15 ॰

O GOD, source of the Light that never fades, and of the Life that never ends, apart from whom all is darkness and death; we lift our dimmed faces to Thee, and long for Thy life to flow through our wearied hearts.

To some of us this mortal life has brought no happiness or lasting joy; though we sought it long and earnestly. The things on which we set our hearts have faded to shadows in our grasp. The things we dreamed to do we have left all undone, and we are very desolate. Before the gaze of men we have dissembled our weariness and our unrest; but we cannot here. It relieves our spirits, O our Father, to confess what we are; most of us are disappointed and in despair.

We have tried the broad, well-trodden way; and we have found ourselves at last in the wilderness alone, the wine of life turned to gall, its bread to ashes, our hearts weighed down with weariness and sick with fears.

We feel there is something in life we have missed, we feel it as we look toward the western sky, feel it beneath the quiet stars, feel it most of all when we see what Jesus made of life like ours.

Can we retrace our steps and seek the cross-ways once again where long ago we missed our path? Dimly we remember there a narrow way led upward to a place called Golgotha, where, beyond, we saw the sky break clear upon a city's towers.

O Shepherd of the lost, lead us there again; and if the returning way be too hard, and long, and sad for us to bear, of Thy great love lift us up and carry us, like the lambs, upon Thy shoulders. Amen.

16

O GOD, we have heard of Thee with the hearing of the ear, but we want to know Thee for ourselves. We touch the outskirts of Thy presence, but we desire to see Thee face to face. We believe Thou art guiding our lives, but we want to feel Thy hand.

But ah, how purely we must love the truth if we are ever to know Thee; and it is this that makes us fear we never may. Despite all our earnestness and bravery, we are fearful lest the truth should overturn some beloved and sheltering lie. We are curious to know the hidden truth of things, but we dread to learn the truth about ourselves.

How deeply we must hunger after righteousness if we would see Thy kingdom come. We long for righteousness, but mostly in those who have wronged us, and in the ordering of things without. If it should mean a reformation of our lives, some great renunciation of ourselves, we fear our love for righteousness might never stand the strain.

We remember that to love Thee we must love our brother also; and this we were prepared to do till someone we despised or hated crossed our path, and then what seemed the easy way to Thee became impossible.

Yet, O Most Merciful, heed not our fears, consider not our cowardice, forgive our failings. But hearken to those prayers of our hearts which come to us in highest moments

when we forget ourselves and think of Thee.
Amen.

17

O THOU who hast visited the children of men with Thy presence, and hast made us conscious of our ignorance, sin and frailty; either take away our hopes or satisfy us early with Thy mercy. A spark disturbs our clod; O free us from its plague, or fan it into flame until all dross and earthiness are consumed.

Righteousness we cannot claim, yet we hunger for it, and can endure no longer that our hunger go unsatisfied. Why hast thou wakened our discontent, if not to lead us higher? Remain as we are we cannot; either sink beneath where pain is not, or rise above where pain is turned to purity, we must; yet neither can we seem to do.

O leave us not; not for all our complainings, nor for any pain. Better thirst and famine, tears and torment, than the comfortable sleep of death.

Is this longing but Thyself? Then come, our God, as cleansing wind, as flaming fire, O come quickly. Amen.

18 ❧

O GOD, who hast made all things, and orderest all things to fulfill Thy purposes; we whom Thou hast created to be free and choose the good, turn again to Thee; for our freedom is found only in Thy service, and there is no good that we desire beside Thee.

It cannot be that Thou hast created what Thou canst not govern, yet we have been strangely willful and rebellious. We have wrestled all night with one who would overcome us, and then in the morning light have seen Thy face and learned Thy name. We have closed our door against an entreating voice, to find that light and joy have departed from us.

Surely Thou wilt not leave us because we fought against Thee; we did not know with whom we strove. Take not our refusal for an answer, but have pity on our misguided minds.

Can it be that Thou hast created a capacity that Thou canst not satisfy, that these hearts must for ever hunger and never be filled, these eyes strain to watch for a glory that they can never behold? O God, none but Thyself, none but Thyself; not Thy gifts, but Thee we crave.

Thus we lift to Thee our broken cries, come to us through the night, and bid us be not afraid. O come. Amen.

❧ THE INNER COURT

I called upon the Lord in distress: the Lord answered me, and set me in a large place.

—*Psalm 118:5*

O GOD, too near to be found, too simple to be conceived, too good to be believed; help us to trust, not in our knowledge of Thee, but in Thy knowledge of us; to be certain of Thee, not because we feel our thoughts of Thee are true, but because we know how far Thou dost transcend them. May we not be anxious to discern Thy will, but content only with desire to do it; may we not strain our minds to understand Thy nature, but yield ourselves and live our lives only to express Thee.

Turn us back from our voyages of thought to that which sent us forth. Lead us out of confusion to simplicity. Call us back from wandering without to find Thee at home within.

Amen.

20 ટ✦

O MOST Merciful, whose love to us is mighty, long-suffering, and infinitely tender; lead us beyond all idols and imaginations of our minds to contact with Thee the real and abiding; past all barriers of fear and beyond all paralysis of failure to that furnace of flaming purity where falsehood, sin and cowardice are all consumed away. It may be that we know not what we ask; yet we dare not ask for less.

Our aspirations are hindered because we do not know ourselves. We have tried to slake our burning thirst at broken cisterns, to comfort the crying of our spirits with baubles and trinkets, to assuage the pain of our deep unrest by drugging an accusing conscience, believing a lie, and veiling the naked flame that burns within. But now we know Thou makest us never to be content with aught save Thyself, in earth, or heaven, or hell.

Sometimes we have sought Thee in agony and tears, scanned the clouds and watched the ways of men, considered the stars and studied the moral law; and returned from all our search no surer and no nearer. Yet now we know that the impulse to seek Thee came from Thyself alone, and what we sought for was the image Thou hadst first planted in our hearts.

We may not yet hold Thee fast or feel Thee near, but we know Thou holdest us, and all is well. Amen.

O GOD, infinite in Mercy, Love, and Power, hear the cry of Thy children, meet our deep necessities, and answer our unutterable desires.

We come to Thee as those who are brought sick and wasted to their native air, when all other cures have failed. Thou hast made us, and stood us a hand's-breadth off, that we might return to Thee if we chose; and because we did not know, and were childish and willful, we essayed to managed life alone.

We have failed to comprehend ourselves or grasp our little life's full meaning. We bring Thee but broken aspirations, unfulfilled attempts, and many a failure that makes us ashamed. Wilt Thou receive us? The night is coming down dark and fearful, there is no time to put things straight, and our eyes are aching for the light.

Thou didst send us into life infants without knowledge, but full of needs. There was so much that promised to satisfy: the bauble of fame, the glitter of gold, the seductiveness of sin. When these had failed we tried the waters of forgetfulness, and the bread of pleasure; and now famine has come, and we perish here with hunger.

Father we remember still the house where even the servants had enough and to spare, and we turn our steps homeward again. Meet us with the kiss of peace. Amen.

22 ⧉

ALMIGHTY Father, whose presence fillest all things; we thank Thee that Thou canst by no means be excluded from the work of Thy hands. We thank Thee that Thou hast made us to realize Thyself, and that Thy purposes are beyond defeat. We have shut ourselves in, girded the mind with strong argument, repeated our unbelief like a creed, but we have never escaped Thee.

We have striven to walk alone in pride, sufficiency and ostentation, and then some thought of Thee has shattered all our wilfulness and we have gone softly ever afterward, and prayed: God be merciful to me a sinner.

We have plunged into sin, we have turned from the bright ideals which plagued us, we have stabbed at our own complaining souls, drugged our conscience, poisoned our minds, set up idols, made our hearts like hell—and lo, Thou art there.

We yield to Thee, O God, for Thou art stronger than we. We cannot escape Thee without forsaking our reason, our hope and our joy. We cannot do without Thee, unless we surrender all that comforts and all that inspires. Forgive us our folly, pardon our wandering, make room for us within Thy gracious love. Amen.

MERCIFUL Father, whose faithfulness abides all our fickleness whose forgiveness outlasts all our sins; take from our minds, we pray, the delusions that threaten our sanity and mislead our minds. We mistake shadows for realities, we are afraid of things that do not exist, we spend our labor for bread that perisheth, for treasures that fade.

Reveal to us wherein standeth our life, lest we miss for ever its significance and reality, and it pass like a dream away.

Be gracious to us, O Compassionate, when with the light shining clear upon us we turn in madness and rebellion to the dark. Why should we fall so easily and turn away so soon? Help us to believe that in all our sin and self-reproach Thou abidest with us still, and that our sorrow is but Thyself suffering within to bring us to salvation.

We turn in longing unto Thee; Thy perfection calls us, Thy mercy welcomes us. Be unto us as the morning, dear Grace of God. Be unto us as fires that cleanse, Thou glorious Sun of Righteousness. Amen.

24 ૭➤

ALMIGHTY God, in whom alone we live, we turn in all our need to Thee, the fountain of our life. Thou hast made all things dependent upon Thee for their existence, and Thou hast made our hearts so that they fail without the inspiration of Thy presence. Forgive us if, knowing this, we have been careless about that which should be our chief concern, if we have taken no pains to establish a life of communion with Thee, if we have not hungered and thirsted after righteousness. We have been slack in prayer, careless in living, until we have found a glory departing from the earth and Thy rest from our hearts. We thank Thee that Thou dost never withdraw Thyself from us without our knowing that the Spirit of God has departed. Thou makest us quickly to cry after Thee. O visit us early with Thy mercy, satisfy with Thyself, for Thou art our God. Bind us to Thee with the bond of an endless love. Find us in the wilderness, lead us to where fountains of living waters flow, shepherd us where flowers for ever bloom. Bring us in sight, most Gracious One, of the Cross, at once life's mystery and life's healing. And may our foolish wandering and false self-worship come to an end this day. Hold us, for Thou art stronger than we. Forgive us, for Thou art kinder than we dare to be. Amen.

ETERNAL and ever blessed God, blessed because Thou eternally givest; we thank Thee for the enrichment of our life by the wondrous communication of Thyself to man. We thank Thee that Thou hast set eternity in our hearts and planted the image of Thyself within. We mourn our concern for transient and trifling things which so often distract our minds from high pursuits and set our thoughts upon unworthy ends; yet we are thankful that nothing temporal has power to satisfy our souls. We lament the defacement of Thine image in us by foolish sin and irreverent thought, but we rejoice that it can never quite be blotted out. For Thou hast made the world without us and the heart within to bring these things continually to mind. The murmur of the wind, the far-stretching distance, the purple mountains set the spirit longing for something vaster than earth itself can give. The love of friends, the inner vision of the soul, the spur of conscience, and the commanding call of goodness keep Thine image bright within.

For all our failures and our faithlessness Thou art still our hope. Cast us not away from Thy presence, and take not Thy Holy Spirit from us. Amen.

26 ३०

SOUL of the universe, Light of the mind of man, Spirit of Jesus Christ; who dwellest in all things, from whom and in whom and unto whom we are; we thank Thee that Thou hast so formed the world and so made the heart of man that we cannot escape Thee and would not if we could.

In all our restless desire it is Thee we really seek, even though we know it not; for if we have all and not Thee, we have nothing, and our spirits remain still famished and athirst.

Thou comest to us through every channel of impression and visitest the heart in every experience; for even though we do not mark Thy coming and we fail to recognize Thy hand ever and always Thou findest some secret way within, and the silence of the soul announceth Thou art there.

Interpret then to us, we pray Thee, the movement of the world and the motives of our hearts; so that we shall no longer search for what we have, nor seek with sin to stay desires designed to find no satisfaction till we come to Thee.

Shine through our blindness, break through all our delusions, strive with our rebellion, plead with our pride. Thou art our All, leave us not. Amen.

O GOD, whose word is hidden in the framework of the world, shines in the mind of man, and is made flesh in Jesus Christ; we have heard Thee calling us by name, and like sheep to a shepherd, children to a father, we come to Thee.

In every age men have heard Thy voice, and we can hear it still. We have journeyed far, but Thy voice has followed; we have been careless, rebellious, and sometimes tried to drown Thy call; but as we dared to hearken, it came back again, and is with us to this hour.

We know we can never roam where that voice will not follow, nor shall we ever try again; for we know it leads to joy and rest, to happy service and to perfect freedom. We know it is the voice of love beyond imagination or desire, the call of a heart that feels and cares.

So long, so late, and many of us so sad, yet at last we come. Fold us with Thy ~~sleep,~~ sheep number us among Thy family, call us to be Thy friends. Amen.

28 ৰ২

O INFINITE Light of Truth, dawn upon our darkened minds, and lead us past all shams and shadows to Thyself. Make us discontented with anything less than Thee, lest we be found following broken lights or moulding some image of Thee from base desire.

O Infinite Life of Love, the Source, the Way, the Goal of all true life; may we feel the tides of Thy Being sweeping round our hearts, catch sight of that immortal sea which brought us hither, and open the flood-gates of our lives to the ocean of Thy love.

Forgive us for our shrinking from the light, forgive us for all fear of love. Leave us not alone to our darkness and dread, lift up our hearts and make us strong. Amen.

O THOU who art all, without Thee we are nothing; yet Thou who art all can surely make us something. To live apart from Thee is impossible; to hate Thee is to court death; to love Thee is to love everything; what shall we do then but love Thee, and all things shall then be ours.

Thy law is inevitable, and Thy love is inescapable. Whither shall we flee from Thy Spirit or whither shall we go from Thy presence? If we ascend to the heavens, Thou art there, and it is Thyself that makest all the hells our souls can know. We have to come to Thee because we cannot fly from Thee; we yield to Thee because we can do no other.

But not only because we must, but because we may, we come to Thee; it is Thy love that compels, and it is our very selves that answer to Thy call. The revelation of Thyself ends all rebellion, the shewing of Thy heart has broken ours. From One who has loved us to the uttermost, we cannot keep our own poor love. To the Father who begat us, and bore with us and desires to be our Friend, we cannot refuse the service of our sonship. So, as an arrow to its mark, as dew drawn heavenward by the sun, as a child to its mother's breast, we come.

Amen.

30 ⁊

O GOD, who hast encompassed us with so much that is dark and perplexing, and yet hast set within us light enough to walk by; enable us to trust what Thou hast given as sufficient for us, and steadfastly refuse to follow aught else; lest the light that is in us become as darkness and we wander from the way. May we be loyal to all the truth we know, and seek to discharge those duties which lay their commission of our conscience; so that we may come at length to perfect light in Thee, and find our wills in harmony with Thine.

Since Thou has planted our feet in a world so full of chance and change that we know not what a day may bring forth, and hast curtained every day with night and rounded our lives with sleep; grant that we may work while it is called day, since the night cometh when no man can work.

Since we are so feeble, faint and foolish, leave us not to our own devices, not even when we pray Thee to; nor suffer us, to walk our own unheeding way. Plant thorns about our feet, touch our hearts with fear, give us no rest apart from Thee, lest we lose our way and miss the happy gate. Amen.

O LORD most high and wonderful, to whose mind the past and the future meet in our eternal now, to whose sight all things lie naked and open; we are the creatures of shifting time to whom the past is soon forgotten and from whom the future is completely veiled.

Our day is but a gleam of light between two nights of dark. The mists hang about our minds, our feet are fettered, we are bruised and bound, robbed and cheated every day. Yet we can conceive a higher knowledge beside which ours is poor and incomplete. Though our ignorance is well-nigh universal, at least we know we do not know; our night is never so long or so dark that we forget what the day is like. We are more than we seem, and Thou art nearer than we dream. Yet we only dare to ask for light upon one step ahead, faith to take one day at a time, endurance to wait for the dawn.

Forgive the crushing care that comes from our lack of vision, our fears that the truth will never be clear, our frenzied, ineffectual strivings. Let us feel through all that Thou dost lead us on. Forgive the impertinence that would hurry on the dawn, that would thrust impious hands across the pattern. Thou art weaving, that would outrun Thy perfect will for us.

May we become heirs to the Spirit of Jesus,

confident that the truth shall yet be proclaimed from the housetops, courageous enough to endure the cross, despise the shame, and in death to commit ourselves into Thy hands. Amen.

32 ⁊

O GOD, the Author of all joy, and the ground of all gladness; we thank Thee that life is to be crowned at last with song.

Sometimes we find it hard to believe that when the world began the sons of God shouted for joy, so mournful has proved the course of the world; and harder still to believe that the song of the redeemed shall overwhelm in its richness and beauty, the song of the unsinning angels.

We bring our broken lives to Thee, and pray Thee make all our lives a hymn of praise.
Amen.

O THOU who art from everlasting to everlasting, Ancient of days, yet ever new; all things wax old as doth a garment, but Thou art the same and Thy years shall not fail. We who are born amid the things of time and swaddled in a vesture of sense, turn to catch some glimpse of things eternal. Our life is but a moment in the vastness of eternity, and yet it is long enough for us to grow old and care-worn. We inherit wisdom from all the ages, the key of hidden treasure is in our hands, but we do not understand the truth; we are very wise but very weary; rich and increased with goods, but friendless and unloved. We have spoiled our sight in poring over many books, while the unclasped books of nature and the heart remain unread. And now, like men of old, we have come to search for simplicity, for freedom and for truth. Lead us, O Father, back to the lowliness of childhood, that we may be born again. Lead us to the Babe of Bethlehem, to Thy Holy Child Jesus, to Him who kept His heart unaged through all His years of earth, and is now alive for evermore.

Carry us in Thy arms as a child; as a mother comforteth her only son, so comfort us; for with all our years and learning we are infants crying in the night, hungry for the breast of God. Amen.

34 ॐ

STANDING, O our God, upon the shrinking shores of time, where ever break and moan the waves of an eternal sea, we feel utterly homeless and afraid. Beneath our feet, crumbling rock and shifting sand; around us, scenes that change; before us, an ocean perilous, unchartered and dark with storm. We have heard that far over the horizon islands of the blest lift fronded palms in air. All we know for certain is that this is not our home. We cannot stand this restless change, this hurrying pace of life, the loss of loved ones, the terror of the shade which creeps around us. We must build our everlasting mansion, not here upon time's flooded shore but in Thee, man's dwelling-place in every generation.

Standing, O our God, before the face of Christ so glorious, beneath His cross so strange, we cannot rest content with what we are, so craven, mean and petty, so sinful, stained and poor. We know we were meant to be infinitely more. Thy voice in Him calls us to live as sons of God, to venture all, to love to the uttermost, to spend ourselves even unto death. But the flesh is weak; our frailty shrinks from His purity, His loneliness, His awful Passion. Yet if we could only be as He, we should be at last at rest. Then, O reveal Thy Son in us. May Christ be born within us, and rise from the tomb of our dead selves, glorious and triumphant Amen.

O THOU, whose love passeth knowledge, and whose peace passeth understanding, it was Thy thought which conceived us, Thy love which bare us. We are of yesterday and know nothing, and yet we partake of Thine infinite nature; the truth we cannot attain shines ever before us, so that we know how far short of Thy glory we fall. Our hearts are restless in their search for rest, and even though we find nothing to satisfy our desire, this but witnesses that Thou Thyself art the goal of all our strivings; it is Thyself who hast made us to long for Thine infinite perfection, Thy eternal nature, Thy holy and omnipotent love.

We thank Thee for the unquenchable impulse toward Thee Thou hast planted within. We are pained by its passion, disturbed by its desire, and there have been times when we have sought to destroy its power; but we thank Thee we cannot.

We bless Thee for Him who gave full utterance to Thy Spirit, whose joy was to do Thy will, who clothed the inborn word with flesh, that all might come to know themselves and Thee. We see Thy purpose for our life on earth displayed in Christ, and we would yield our spirits to Him; but Thy purpose for our life to come is lost in unimaginable glory and light.

Set us in the light of eternity once again

today. Reveal what we are. Make us able to bear Thy revelation, brave enough to do Thy will. Enable us to see the path that leads to Thee, in the things around us; to respond to Thy call to holy, helpful service. O give us to express something of Thee before we go hence and on our life's brief day the night comes down. Amen.

36 ह~

IMMORTAL, Eternal, Invisible, with whom is no mutability or changing shade, no night or winter, no ebbing tide; we, the children of time and sense, are met to worship Thee. Thou art the same yesterday, today, and for ever, and we are fretted by every passing wind, tempest-tossed and afraid. Thy years fail not, and though all things fade as doth a garment, Thou remainest; while we spend our years as a tale that is told. Thy holiness and perfection surpass all thought, and we are stained by childish faults and petty sins.

Make us not to despair, Eternal Father; we are called by Thy name, we are Thine. Thou hast set thoughts of Thee in our hearts, Thou hast made us restless among the things we see, Thou hast made us to thirst after purity, Thou hast taught us to hope for eternal life.

Teach us not to despise the life we are called to live, since it was given us by Thee. Teach us not to neglect the task of today because we cannot see its eternal effect. Teach us not to neglect the little duties which are training us for a great stewardship. May we remember that this life of ours has been divinely lived, that this robe of flesh and strange infirmity has been Thy garment: Teach us so to live that we may not fear the judgment of the world to come, nor be frightened at the flaming of eternal dawn. Amen.

37

O FATHER, who hast ordained that we be set within a scheme of circumstance, and that in stern conflict we should find our strength and triumph over all; withhold not from us the courage by which alone we ran conquer. Still our tongues of their weak complainings, steel our hearts against all fear, and in joyfully accepting the conditions of our earthly pilgrimage may we come to possess our souls and achieve our purposed destiny.

It has pleased Thee to hide from us a perfect knowledge, yet Thou callest for a perfect trust in Thee. We cannot see tomorrow, we know not the way we take, darkness hangs about our path and mystery meets us at every turn. Yet Thou hast shut us up to final faith in goodness, justice, truth; that loving these for themselves alone, we may find the love that passeth knowledge, and look upon Thy face.

O suffer us not for any terror of darkness or from any torment of mind to sin against our souls, or to fail at last of Thee. Amen.

O GOD, who hast sent us to school in this strange life of ours, and hast set us tasks which test all our courage, trust and fidelity; may we not spend our days complaining at circumstance or fretting at discipline, but give ourselves to learn of life and to profit by every experience. Make us strong to endure.

We pray that when trials come upon us we may not shirk the issue or lose our faith in Thy goodness, but committing our souls unto Thee who knowest the way that we take, come forth as gold tried in the fire.

Grant by Thy grace that we may not be found wanting in the hour of crisis. When the battle is set, may we know on which side we ought to be, and when the day goes hard, cowards steal from the field and heroes fall around the standard, may our place be found where the fight is fiercest. If we faint, may we not be faithless; if we fall, may it be while facing the foe. Amen.

39 ào

O THOU, who turnest the shadow of death into the morning, and makest the day dark with night, to whom darkness and light are both alike, come and abide with us through every experience of life. The day is Thine when shines the sun and all our path is fair; the night is Thine when stars light up the vastness of Thy world. Help us neither to weary of the day, nor fear what night may bring.

Sometimes we turn from the certitude that we have in Thee, to follow vain shadows again, and bring upon ourselves anguish and confusion; but Thou knowest where we are, and at our faintest cry of need the valleys are exalted. every hill made low, and a straight path runs before us to Thyself.

When, perverse and foolish, we leave the pleasant paths of peace, taste the bitterness of sin, fall into the mire, and come at length to loathe ourselves; Thine amazing love brings Thee over the mountains of our misery, into the wilderness where we have wandered; seeks until it finds, clasps us again, bears us in Thy strong embrace, and brings us home rejoicing.

Oh the depth of Thy mercy, and the wonder of Thy love! Amen.

OUR ETERNAL Father, whose kindness is loving and whose mercy is tender, we come to cast ourselves upon Thee, for Thou hast made us, We rest in the thought that Thy love knows no end nor change, else it would not love us long. Our love knows so little constancy, it changes with our moods, it proves worthless in the hour of trial. We need to know that Thou art long-suffering and Thy patience endless, for we soon lose patience with ourselves. We are so spoilt by prejudice, so blinded by pride, so dense to the simplest things. We are burdened by things that do not matter, bewildered by problems of our own imagination, fearful at that which does not exist. Thou hast made heirs of all the ages, we stand at the confluence of time, and yet in many ways we fall beneath the measure of the men who went before us. Our vision is wider, but our enthusiasm less; our knowledge deeper, but our peace less secure; and we incline to blame the knowledge and the vision, instead of ourselves.

We pray for strength for our burdens, wisdom for our responsibilities, insight for our times, faith enough for the wider demand. Our God, make us strong, make us strong.

Pardon all our littleness, our foolishness, our distrust, our fickleness of spirit. Give us breadth like the sea, constancy like Christ's, the love that passeth knowledge, the peace that passeth understanding. Amen.

41 ଽ᷾

O GOD, who remainest the same though all else fades, who changest not with our changing moods, who leavest us not when we leave Thee; we thank Thee that when we lose faith in Thee, soon or late we come to faith in something that leads us back again with firmer trust and more security. Even if we wander into the far country we take ourselves with us; ourselves who are set toward Thee as rivers to the sea. If we turn to foolishness, our hearts grow faint and weary, our path is set with thorns, the night overtakes us, and we find we have strayed from light and life.

Grant to us clearer vision of the light which knows no shade of turning, that we stray not in folly away; incline our hearts to love the truth alone, so that we miss Thee not at last; give us to realise of what spirit we are, so that we cleave ever to Thee, who alone can give us rest and joy. Amen.

O GOD, in whom we live and move and have our being, enable us to feel the strength that surrounds us, to follow the light that indwells us, and to avail ourselves of the wisdom Thou givest liberally to all who ask of Thee.

Give to us so great a love of truth that we may pass beyond all doubt and error, until our minds are stayed on Thee, and our thoughts are kept in perfect peace.

Give us wisdom to follow the promptings of duty in our daily lives, that we may grow conscious of Thy presence who workest hitherto, and callest us to be fellow workers now with Thee.

Grant unto us the grace of penitence that we may not grow insensible to our need of forgiveness, from one another, and from Thee; but seek cleansing in communion, fellowship in the light, and rest upon Thy heart. Amen.

43 ह**◆**

OUR FATHER, these words concerning the Eternal City most strangely move our hearts. No such city have we ever seen, and yet the story of its painless, unshadowed day, its crystal streams, its healing trees, makes us think of home. Some thought of such a habitation where we could dwell in light for evermore, and separation, night and sorrow should be done away, has often stirred within us; and then the fairest cities of earth have seemed to us like cities of dreadful night.

We have dared to hope that this heaven of our heart's desire shall one day be our own. We have even dreamed that here on earth we might help to build that city's walls.

But there has come to us the awful fear that we could have no place in such a city. Our hostile spirits, our bitter tempers, our selfish hearts would play the traitor to any commonwealth of the soul. Heaven could never lie about us, while hell burned within the heart. And yet we cannot be content to take our place with those who miss the gate and wander in the outer darkness, homeless and hardening in hate.

Our only hope, O Holy One, is in Thy willingness to dwell with us, till we are fit to dwell in Thee, Thou only City of the soul.

Amen.

MOST Merciful and Compassionate Father, Thou knowest our nature and readest our inmost thoughts, and nothing can be hidden from Thee; help us then to unburden ourselves of every disguise we wear before the face of man, and find rest in being what we are and nothing more. Enable us to put off all sham and pretense, so that from henceforth we may live a life of freedom and sincerity. Be patient with any of us who still prefer vain shows and empty pride to the shelter and refuge of truth. Leave us not utterly alone when at length we face the disillusionment of life; when our dearest hopes fade away and ambition fails us, be Thou nigh, nor of Thy goodness leave us to despair.

We feel that Thy sheltering love has been about us all our days, wooing us to better things, but we are conscious that ofttimes we have done despite to Thy grace, and our foolish hearts have spurned the only Love that would stoop to such as we. If Thy goodness were not infinitely patient, and Thy love were not stronger than our stubbornness, we were all lost and undone.

When, disappointed with ourselves, sickened with our sin, worsted by life, and wounded by the world, we turn to Thee; though late the hour and fled life's little day, reject us not, for pity's sake. Amen.

45 ॐ

AS we have come into this place of prayer, out of darkness into light, out of the drear night into the shelter of home, out of our loneliness into the fellowship of the saints, so may we come, O God, to Thee; from all cloud and shadow, from all falsehood and un-reality, to truth, to certainty, to the welcome of Thine arms and the shining of Thy face.

May no indocility of temper, no indolence of mind, no perversity of spirit cloud the vision of Thyself, or bar our breast against Thine entering in. May we dare to leave the door upon the latch to Truth, to Christ, to Thee.

Thou knowest all the unhappiness of our life, its weariness, sadness and strain, the feeling that no one cares, that the game is nearly done, and life can hold no more light and comfort for us. If Thou hast nothing more to give, we are of all men most miserable.

Make known to us, we pray, the blessed-ness of those who serve Thee, the joy of the Cross, the rest of those who wear Christ's easy yoke, and may we be comforted and made glad. Grant us to that last great grace of life which transforms all things and renews the soul: the sense of Thy friendship and nearness, a hand in ours, a companion on the weary way, a light within the heart. So redeem the days we have wasted, reveal the meaning of the life we have so nearly lost, lift from us the melancholy of our mistakes, and turn all our mourning into joy. Amen.

46 ह>

IMMORTAL, Eternal, Invisible, who hidest Thyself in darkness and silence, who veilest Thy glory in the lesser beauty of nature; Thy form is unknown, Thy name we mortals dare not utter; yet Thy worship is truth and Thy tabernacle man. Calm our passions, silence our clamorous thoughts, that we may be still and know that Thou art God. Put out all lesser lights that we may see the Light within. Naked in soul we stand before Thy dread tribunal, that, trembling there, we may know no other fear; that gazing upon the face of the Eternal we may not fear the face of man. Lead us through the deeps of our own nature, past the gateways of thought, till face to face, heart to heart, thought to thought, we are in Thy presence.

Break down pride, burn out sin, banish self. May perfect love cast out all fear, perfect sacrifice make an end of sin, and Thou, the All in all, smite down the prison house of self and set our spirits free, in tune with the Infinite, at home with the Eternal. Shut us in with Thyself, O God. Amen.

47 ह

O SHEPHERD of Israel, who dost neither slumber nor sleep, we are the people of Thy pasture and the sheep of Thy hand. Fold us safely in Thy love, lest we be overtaken by the storm and be lost in the darkness. And if in carelessness, or curiosity or willful pride, we should wander from Thy care, O leave us not, good Shepherd, to our fate, but seek us till Thou findest us, and bear us home again.

Thou knowest the rebellion that often rules our will, the instinct to rove, the desire for strange scenes and the thirst for adventure. How little we understand that the fold is freer than the plain, following Thee more adventurous than wandering at will, and what in Thee seems to us unreason and austerity, only Thy perfect knowledge of what we need, a love for us that passes understanding.

Pardon the evil thoughts we think of Thee, and grant to us wisdom and repentance. Make us to love Thy voice and answer to the name by which Thou callest us; suffer us not to fall from Thy guidance, and may no one pluck us from Thy hand.

Beside the still waters, through the green pastures, and in the valley where dark shadows lie, be Thou our strength and shield, and may we come to find even thy rod and Thy staff a stay and comfort to us. So shepherd us beyond the plains of peril to the eternal fold, where we may lie down in safety, and go in and out freely for evermore. Amen.

48 ࿔

O GOD, the Source of our being, the Goal of our desire, and the Guide of these our pilgrim days; we have turned aside from the ceaseless fret of life that we may think of all it means for us. We would stay for a moment the noisy shuttle of time, that we may watch the pattern it is weaving. We would hush our busy thoughts, that we might learn in silence the mysteries of our being.

Beyond the clouds that veil our sight, we feel the sun must still be shining; behind the tangle of human affairs some mighty purpose working, beneath the strange yearnings of our souls there moves Thyself, awful, vast and holy. Gleams of purpose have visited our minds, the sense of some great destiny accompanies all our thoughts. We have reason for believing Thou art nearer than we think.

O God, our Life, our Hope, our Strength; leave us not. Make us sure of Thee. Disclose Thy purposes. Make Thy way straight before us. Amen.

49 ౿

GRACIOUS Father of our spirits, in the stillness of this worship may we grow more sure of Thee, who art often closest to us when we feel Thou hast forsaken us. The toil and thought of daily life leave us little time to think of Thee; but may the silence of this holy place make us aware that though we may forget Thee, Thou dost never forget us. Perhaps we have grown careless in contact with common things, duty has lost its high solemnities, the altar fires have gone untended, Thy light within our minds has been distrusted or ignored. As we withdraw awhile from all without, may we find Thee anew within, until thought grows reverent again, all work is hallowed, and faith reconsecrates all common things as sacraments of love.

If pride of thought and careless speculation have made us doubtful of Thee, recover for us the simplicity that understands Thou are never surer than when we doubt Thee, that through all failures of faith Thou becomest clearer, and so makest the light that once we walked by seem but darkness. Help us then to rest our faith on the knowledge of our imperfection, our consciousness of ignorance, our sense of sin, and see in them shadows cast by the light of Thy drawing near.

If Thy purposes have crossed our own and Thy will has broken ours, enable us to trust the wisdom of Thy perfect love and find Thy will to be our peace.

So lead us back to meet Thee where we may have missed Thee. Amen.

50 ৪৯

O GOD, the Light of all that is true, the Strength of all that is good, the Glory of all that is beautiful, we thank Thee that Thou hast put within our minds some spark of the eternal flame, some desire after goodness, some enjoyment of whatsoever things are lovely.

We thank Thee for the strength of reason and for all the inner kingdom of the mind; for every thought that lifts us to Thyself; for every noble desire; for every holy impulse.

We thank Thee that Thou hast so framed our hearts that our deepest instincts anchor us to Thee: that Thou hast so created everything, that he who loves the Truth can never miss Thee at the last. In all our thoughts, save us from anxiety, presumption, and fear. Deliver us from all faleshood, error, and prejudice. And as we have gathered ourselves to seek Thee afresh may all our doubts vanish before the shining of Thy face, and as our thoughts are hushed to silence now, may we find Thee moving upon our minds, higher than our highest thought, yet nearer to us than our very selves. Inspire, uplift, and comfort us, and manifest Thyself, O God. Amen.

O GOD and Father of us all, breathe upon us now Thine hallowed calm; lift the burden from our hearts, soothe the anxieties of our minds, and send peace into our souls.

Forgive the disorder, the fever, the vain purpose of our lives. We have made haste as those who believe not. We have been desperate as those who lead a forlorn hope; we have not trusted in Thee who workest evermore. We have spent our days contrary to Thy plainest laws. Our eyes have been fixed to earth, and rarely lifted to the hills. We have not silenced ourselves to hear, nor been patient to understand. We have been fretful as children, comfortless as those who never knew Thee. We have spent our strength on things that do not profit, and labored for the bread that perisheth; while Thy free and glorious gifts have lain near to us unappropriated and often spurned.

Help us now to stand awhile in the shelter of Thy shadowing wings, and to be still; to look out again upon life with new vision, that we may understand; to wait for the revelation of Thy will that shall make us calm and strong. Amen.

52 ⧉

OUR Father, tempest-tossed and worn with war, we turn to Thee in deepest need. Without, all is tumult and confusion; within, weariness and deep dispeace. The storm has left us tired with watching, the strife has found out every weakness, and we long to be at rest.

We want rest; yet not the rest of those who sit with idle hands, not the rest of those who cease from mental strife, not the rest of those whose ambitions leave them disillusioned or content. We want that inward rest of soul which comes to those who share the easy yoke of Christ.

We need forgiveness; nought else can meet our case. The struggle has not left us unscarred, our souls are disfigured and stained, and sin has enfeebled our will. Yet no easy word of pardon, Lord, or promise of forgetfulness; not merely the hiding of Thine eyes or a garment to cover our shame; nothing but the transformation of our being, the cleansing of the heart by blood, the weaving of a robe of righteousness from repentance and renewed desire.

We need a refuge, for the tempest still is high. Yet not a refuge from life, from truth, from Thee. We want to face life with strength for all realities; we want to find our refuge only in the truth; we want to hide ourselves deep within Thy heart. Amen.

O GOD, who art so near that nearer Thou cannot be, whose Spirit mingles with our own as sunshine in the air; even this does not content us, unless we can feel Thy presence and see Thy light and look upon Thy face.

We know Thou art in our minds, yet Thou art always a step beyond our thoughts; and we long to speak with Thee as friend with friend. In the stillness of the chamber, under the silence of the stars, we know Thou art; but oh that Thou couldst call us as a mother calls her child. We believe Thou art near, for suddenly our hearts grow still, heavenly thoughts stir within the mind, in sad and lonely hours we smile and know not why; but oh that we could feel Thee like the wind upon our cheeks, like the tide about the shore, like a hand within our own.

We could understand Thy love if it were warm with our own humanity, we could even dare to love Thee if Thou wouldst clothe Thyself in our frail form; we could trust ourselves to life if Thou couldst consent to walk our ways, endure our sorrows, and taste the bitterness of death. Amen.

54 ઠ✎

O THOU who art more truly than can be thought, and who can be thought more truly than uttered, silence seems the only worship we can bring. We call Thee holy, but how poor is all our thought of holiness. Thy name is Love, but how little we know of what love may be. Yet leave us not to worship Thee dumbly and perplexed; rather come to us in kindling thought, and open our lips to shew forth Thy praise. Stoop to our world of sense that we may be lifted to comprehend Thine ineffable nature. We thank Thee that high as Thou art, Thou hast buried within us thoughts of Thyself: thoughts of infinite and perfect goodness, longings for a holiness that knows no defeat of sin, promptings of a love that puts self to painless death. We thank Thee that in the fulness of time Thou didst gather man's blind thoughts and mingle them with Thine to make the Word Christ Jesus.

Now Thou art near to us, all our sufferings are Thine, our very sins are borne by Thee, and in the mystery of an eternal sacrifice Thou hast atoned us unto Thee, and overcome all sin and separation.

Praise be unto Thee, O Lord most High.

Amen.

O GOD, Thou knowest how our hearts
yearn after Thee. Thou hast heard the prayers which plead for Thee to manifest Thyself
to us. And sometimes it has seemed that there
was none to hear, and none to answer us. For
when we asked to see Thy power, we saw only
a child set in our midst; and we felt we had
been mocked. Yet afterward we saw all the
beasts of the field and all the powers of the
earth led captive by that little child.

We prayed for a revelation of Thy glory,
that we might wonder and worship, and never
doubt again. And then the sunlight failed at
noonday, and outside a city wall a lonely cross
was reared against a darkened sky; and our
very hope became despair. Yet often since we
have seen that cross again, now an ornament
of grace, a holy symbol before which men
bowed, a banner of victory, and a sign of faith.

Men call on Thee to give them light on the
sufferings they are forced to bear, and only the
more does the sense of pain press in upon their
hearts. They find it hard to believe that pain
is the sign of our progress, the promise that
all things shall one day be redeemed. Yet
we thank Thee that Thy revelation is breaking through, and that Thy ways are being
learned.

O Thou, who travailest in us to lead us to a
higher peace, who livest by yielding Thyself to

the uttermost, who are mighty only in mercy, and strong only in humility, reunite us to Thyself, and make Thy perfect will our own.

Amen.

56 &

O GOD, who comest to us disguised in lowliness to seek Thy dwelling with the humble, may false expectations not deceive us, nor pride shut Thee from our hearts.

If Thou comest dressed as Duty, plain, drab and undesired, grant that we may not turn from Thy commands.

If Thou comest robed as Truth, white, relentless and austere, may we not fear to take Thee as our guide.

If Thou comest to us as Love, clothed in flame and crowned with sacrifice, may we not reject the offer of Thyself.

Let us know Thy Name, we pray Thee, lest we be left lamed and lonely to face the light and life of the eternal world. Amen.

O GOD, who cometh to us in an hour when we think not, and in such a way as we least expect; we are all gathered to wait and watch for Thy coming. Disappoint us not because we disappointed Thee when Thou camest to Thine own before. Refuse not to return to us because we knew not the day of Thy visitation, nor the things that belonged to our peace. We had expected a king coming in glory, girt with royal robes; not a wayfaring man who turned aside to tarry for a night. We looked for a mighty conqueror traveling victoriously, who would demand our submission in tones we dared not disobey; not for a suppliant standing at our gate pleading in lowliness and garbed in humility. We awaited one whose raiment would shine like the sun and whose crown was rich with precious stones and purest gold; not one clothed in mockery and crowned with thorns. We sought a Saviour whose magic touch would heal all our sickness, whose medicine would minister to a mind diseased; we never dreamed we might be called to drink a cup of tears and share a baptism of blood.

Yet come again to us. We look no more for seeming strength or outward power, but for a heart which cares, for a face which answers ours. Amen.

58 ह&

O LIGHT Eternal, to whose dawning man lifts his darkened face, shine on us gathered here to wait for Thee. Pierce the earth-born clouds that hide Thee from us, dark clouds of unbelief, chill clouds of anxiety, heavy clouds of despair. May every heart that watches with us see the Sun of Righteousness arise, with healing in His wings.

Pour Thy glory forth that we may see what lies around us. The light in the valley, the rainbow in the storm, the silver lining of the clouds. We thank Thee for the dimmest consciousness of Thy presence; the trail of a seamless robe about us, a light in the sky brighter than that of the sun, a burning of the heart, a whisper in the mind.

But oh for more, for the sunshine of Thy face clear and radiant; the glory of Thy throne resplendent and awful; the majesty of our daily path crowded with helpfulness, broadened with opportunity, a highway through the desert. Oh for that vision for lack of which we perish.

Is this Thy throne, an upreared cross? Is this Thy form, a bleeding Lamb? Ah, Thou hast stricken us, heart-whole, pleasure-loving, by this dying love.

We are humbled, we who never bowed; we are broken, we who never wept; yet let us watch until the mystic sight tells upon our souls, for this is all our life and our salvation.

Amen.

O THOU who are light to all that loves and fire to all that hates, let Thy glory shine upon us, that love in us may come to life and all our hatred be consumed.

O Beauty of ancient days yet ever new, too late have we loved Thee. Our hearts faint for the sight of Thy face, yet when we see Thee we could creep away and hide ourselves for very shame.

O Seeking Saviour of our souls, we could pray Thee to depart from us, for we are sinful men; in Thy pure presence our impurities take on a deeper stain. Yet leave us not, lest we die in our sins.

O Cross that are crimsoned with the cleansing love of God, we would turn away at sight of thee, afraid; yet we want this worn-out self to die, and for the new man created after Christ to rise in power.

Come then again to our hearts: shine upon us in all Thy fairness, burn Thyself ineffaceably within: heal us, though by pain; save us, though by death.

O Man upon Thy cross, we cannot turn back now; for our weakness, pain and need are more than we can bear; Thy sorrow stays our feet, Thy suffering stirs our hearts, Thy sacrifice has saved our souls. O Lamb of God, we come. Amen.

60 ॐ

FATHER, Thou knowest how strangely in us faith and doubt are mingled. Sometimes the darker doubts assail us. Sometimes our hearts are sad with sorrow, and we want no more of life.

Yet now we hear from far-off days a rumor that Jesus has risen from the tomb where He was buried, and showed Himself alive. And as we wait together here we know that it is true. For our hearts are burning with His presence and our faith breaks forth to flame.

Amen.

❧ THE EVENING SACRIFICE

Let my prayer be set forth before
Thee as incense,
and the lifting up of my hands as the
evening sacrifice.

—Psalm 141:2

ETERNAL Father, we come to Thee at the close of day when from olden time men have always turned aside to seek Thy face. With strange rites, by different names, beside cruel altars they made their prayer, and though more light has come to us, and we may have grown wiser than they, our need continues still the same.

We would make to Thee our evensong for the fair beauty of the day, for the Sabbath rest of our spirits, for sacred memories and thoughts of holiness, and for this evening hour made solemn by Thy peace.

Yet we need a peace far deeper than the world can give. For never does departing day find us fit for rest till we have cleansed ourselves by communion with Thee. There haunt us at this hour memories of duties unperformed, promptings disobeyed, deeds of kindness and of pity that we have left too late; words untrue, acts unkind, thoughts impure; the stain of these is on us all. And as the sense of unfading light, of spotless purity, of long-suffering love steals upon us, it makes us all the more ashamed. If this be Thy coming to us, gracious Lord, come nearer still, till selfishness is burned from our breasts, our minds are purged from error, and our wills lose all their weakness in union with Thine own.

Amen.

62 ঽ

ALMIGHTY Father, whose care for us is unsleeping, whose love passeth knowledge, and whose mercy takes away despair; we turn to Thee because apart from Thee we have neither light, nor rest, nor strength. An infinite desire cries out within us that only Thyself can satisfy. We are ashamed for our failures, we chafe at our limitations, we fret within the chains of sin. We feel there is something more for us, and we want to be free. We know there is something higher, and we want to be lifted there.

Come nearer to us than we have ever known. May Thy voice startle us from sleep, may Thy call rouse us from death. If we are living for self, flash in upon our minds the vision of the cross; if we are living carelessly and in sin, may the Christ call us back this night, and whatever we need, do Thou Thyself answer and satisfy. Amen.

O LORD our God, we come at the
close of day to Thee, our Eternal Light, our
refuge in all generations. We thank Thee for
Thy power so unimaginably great, greater
than our failure, our sin, or our rebellion.
Most of all do we thank Thee for the love
which all our foolishness has never tired; the
love which makes all Thy dealings with us
mercy; the love which never despairs; the love
that thinketh on us only for good; the love
that one day shall gather every wanderer
home.

Some of us have grown weary with the heat
and burden of the day. Be a strength and cheer
to us now. Lead us where quiet waters flow.

Some of us have been unfaithful to our great
calling, have slunk from the field in the height
of the conflict, have missed our Leader, blurred
our vision, lost our ideals. Come to us with
visions of victory, nerve us afresh for the fray.

Some of us have been proud and rebellious,
have preferred our own will, loved to see and
choose our path, and are in danger of losing
life, missing the great secret, and laying up for
our selves a harvest of remorse in days to come.
May Thy tender grace soften us, Thy love win
us, the knocking of a pierced hand persuade us
to open the door. Come and abide with us.
Be our guest this night. Nay, take Thy right-
ful place: be the host of our waiting, lonely
hearts. Amen.

64 ୬ঌ

MOST Compassionate Father, whose tender mercy is over all Thy works, we gather ourselves to Thy Name, and seek to realize Thy presence at this evening hour. We are weak, weary, and sinful, but Thou dost know our frame and pitiest our frailties, for Thou didst make us. We bring our sins to Thee, for Thou art gracious and full of compassion, that in the light of Thy face they may melt away.

Receive us, shelter us under Thy wings, hide us in Thy heart. Amen.

O CARE unsleeping, Love unchanging, Light unfading; in Thee is all our strength and hope. If thou didst think no more of us when we thought no more of Thee, how soon we should perish. If Thy love depended on our loveliness, we could hope nothing from Thee. If Thy love was gloomed by our unfaithfulness, how swift and irrevocable our night would be.

Thou art so near us, yet we miss Thee, and often think Thee far away. The path runs straight enough to Thee, yet we lose our way. The knowledge of Thee is clear in us all, yet we are uncertain, and so easily deceived. Thy truth is so simple, and yet it is too hard for us.

We turn to Thee because our feeling of discontent, our sense of sin, our restlessness witness that Thou hast not left us. We silence our thoughts to feel Thee, we hold our eyes to watch for Thee.

Come, as noiseless as the light, and steal within. Brood upon the deep with peace and calm. Touch us with Thy hand that we may turn and see Thy face. Amen.

66 ੩❧

FATHER of Light, Sun of the Soul, when the shadows of twilight fall and darkness ends the day, our thoughts turn to Thee who dwellest where night never comes. It fills us with quiet trust to know that somewhere the truth is always clear, however clouded it appear to us; that there is a light that does not fade when we lose sight of it. Shine through the mists of our mortality and through the deeper gloom of our sin, that the night for us may hold no fears.

If we have lost our way in doubt, so that we despair of Thee, may the light that lighteth every man shine the clearer within us now, and in Thy light may we see light.

And if we have turned aside to try the ways of darkness and death, and fear the light, because of what it may reveal, or hate it because our deeds are evil; yet leave us not, but lead us back by the kindly lights of home, till in Thy flame our sins are consumed and in the light of Thy countenance we rest in peace.

Amen.

O FATHER, we thank Thee for the rest of this sacred day, and for the benediction of the eventide. To every one of us may Thy peace be granted. If the day has been wearying, may the darkness bring refreshing sleep. If any mind has been plagued with perplexity, may there be light for such at evening time. If the quiet of departing day has made us conscious of our sin, may forgiveness fold around us, and may we find the shelter and cleansing of Thy love.

If bitter thoughts, angry clamor and passionate words have disturbed the day of rest, may there creep back into our minds the peace of penitence. If we have closed and barred the door of our hearts against unwelcome truth, may it steal back by secret paths and find its way within.

If we have sought Thee despairingly and think not to have found Thee, may we hear the voice that says: Beloved, thou couldest not have sought Me if I had not found thee.

Amen.

68 ࣿ

O GOD, who from the beginning of the world hast walked with man in the cool of the day, come to commune with us now this eventide, and may no fear or shame lead us to hide ourselves from Thee. Since Thou knowest already our inmost thoughts and beareth still to us a love wherewith we dare not love ourselves, may we consent to walk with Thee in the garden Thou hast planted for our souls.

If any of us have come to the end of this day faint with struggle and worn with failure, confessing ourselves worsted and our strength departed, just as we give up all may we find Thy comfort in our hearts, feel Thy presence at our side, and gird ourselves again for battle.

If any of us have searched for truth till our minds are wearied, and sadness has crept into our eyes, as we relinquish the task and yield ourselves to despair, may we find the light dawning within, and grow sure of Thee who art ever near. Amen.

O FATHER, we are gathered together, a company of men and women, unknown to one another, yet each known to Thee. Some cannot think what has brought them hither: old-time custom, unconscious habit, a desolation in the heart; knowing not that it was Thyself who callest everywhere and movest in all. Some of us are only conscious of our ignorance, aware of the hopeless poverty and confusion of our thoughts. Help us to understand that this is because in the secret places of the mind we touch the wisdom of Thy mighty mind and overhear Thy glorious thoughts. Some of us are saddened and perplexed by the ugliness and misery around us. Help us to understand that this is because we have seen the holy city descending out of heaven. Some of us are in despair because of unworthiness and sin. Grant us to know that only in Thy light could these shadows be discerned.

As stars come out when the sun goes down, strange music sounds when the quiet of evening comes, and voices are heard in the silence which were drowned in the noise of the day, so let us be silent now until Thy presence grows more real and we find both doubt and desire but heralds of Thy drawing nigh. Amen.

70

LORD of the night as of the day, we thank Thee that the gathering darkness so often speaks to us of Thee. It is when the light of day is done that we often grow more conscious of the purer light that shines within. The closing hours of day beget in us a tenderness toward eternal things. A feeling of homelessness moves our feet to seek for Thee, our only rest. The memory of unnoticed sins comes back to mind, and we long for nobler life. We become like the children who put off their garments gladly, who wait to hear again some oft-told tale, who feel they must unburden their hearts to some listening and forgiving heart. Be near us now, O Father.

O Thou, who often standest before us, when for the holding of our eyes we behold Thee not, help us to know Thee near in the darkness of doubt and fear. Save us from despairing of the age that presses round us with its questions and denials, and help us to see in every perplexity of faith but the prelude to some further coming of the Son of Man. Turn us again and cause Thy face to shine upon us, and we shall be saved.

And when we stand within the valley of the shadow and bid a sad farewell to those who journey down its depths alone, or when we ourselves look back for the last time with longing eyes, and then move onward with what hope we may, then let us find what seemed to us such hopeless night only the shadow cast by an eternal dawn. Amen.

71 ࢙

O THOU who companiest with us even when we know it not, shepherdest us in shadowed valleys when we think Thee far away, and often with us sojournest unrecognised; disclose Thyself to us this evening hour, we pray. Apart from Thee all life is joyless, all minds are restless, all hearts loveless. Dare, O Lord, to tabernacle with us, unworthy as we are; and though Thou preferrest before all temples the contrite heart, and grantest only to the pure the vision of Thy face, yet leave us not alone with our pride, nor shrink from contact even with our sin. Only Thy light can make us lowly; the sight of Thee alone will show us what we are. Lift then upon us the light of Thy countenance; draw near and abide with us, for it is toward evening, and the day is far spent. Amen.

72 ౭

OUR GOD, who art the Father of our spirits when evening falls and strange feelings, ancient fears, obstinate questionings, rise within us, we turn to Thee, who alone holdest the secret of Thine own creation.

We believe some kindly purpose lies beyond our coming into the world: not chance, nor fate, nor punishment can explain life; but only love. We feel sure of this because of Thy word in our hearts, and because of Thy Word made flesh.

We have stood before a lonely cross whereon one died, despised and rejected of men, and there we have learned how pain and death need bring no defeat to Thy purposes, and hold no contradiction of Thy love.

Thou hast placed within our trembling hands the strands of life whose issues are in eternity. How shall we live aright; we who are sinful, weak, willful? Be very merciful to Thy children, Father. The lessons of life are difficult unless one interpret to us. Give us tonight Thine interpretation of all that we are, and are destined yet to be. So shall we realize Thy salvation and be glad in Thee all our days.

Amen.

AS the sounds of day die away and the silent night creeps on, may Thy calm, O God, possess our souls. As the storms of passion cease, may our hearts reflect Thy love as the sleeping sea the sky. As our restless thoughts, tired out, give up their fruitless quests, may truth be disentangled in the mind and light shine clear through its untroubled depths.

As the light of sunset fades and the stars steal into the evening sky, so do Thou come into our hearts, noiseless and unheralded, save that we grow conscious Thou art there.

When the instinct of home draws all things that have learned to love, may the turning tide set towards Thee, and may we find ourselves steering for the shore, the Pilot on board, and ere the night comes down, anchored, safe home in port.

We wait, we still our minds, we hush our spirits. Come, gracious Spirit, come. Amen.

74 ತಿ∾

OUR Father, we gather to Thy name as a holy day passes once more in shadow away. Forbid that we should think any day less holy than this, any hour less fleeting. May the solemnity of the hour recall us to the fact that this, like all other days, is the judgment day. May we not be under the delusion that this is not the critical and decisive hour.

May we not fail to recognize Thy presence with us now, and may that open our eyes to Thy presence everywhere. Thou rarely comest to us as King of Kings, as Lord of Lords; but oftenest as truth, or duty, a stranger seeking shelter, a little child, a lonely dying man.

May we not spurn to do the simple thing; to make submission of our spirits, to speak the prayer of our hearts; lest this should be the day of Thy visitation, and we miss the things that belong to our peace. Amen.

FATHER of us all, at this hour when the solitary are set in families, men gather again under the old roof, and wanderers and exiles think longingly of home, we think of Thee the home of us all, of the hearth fire of Thy love where all are welcome, of that last great Christmastide when He who was the Babe of Bethlehem shall have gathered all souls together one unbroken family, not one missing.

May the solemn associations of this hour be blessed to all of us this Christmas Eve. May kind thoughts find lodging in the hardest heart, may longing for purity be born in minds that are unclean, may the lonely and the laboring hear the angels sing tonight.

We are all still children, our Father; our knowledge and our years drop from us all tonight. We gather to Thee, as long ago to our mother's knee. Let us hear again the wonderful story of Thy love, let us listen to the songs of heaven, and in the light of Thy forgiveness have all our doubts and sins and fears dispelled. Amen.

76

OUR GOD, we who are poor and lowly are met to worship Thee the High and Holy. Yet our minds are fearless and our hearts at rest, for in Christ, the holy Child, the Son of Man, the Crucified, Thou hast become to us Immanuel, God for ever with us.

We are gathered for evening prayer, but prayer turns to praise upon our lips, for we have naught to ask of Thee. Thou hast spoken to us so simply, Thou hast come to us so fully, we can never doubt or want again.

The angels sing no more above the cradle of the Christ, but, a greater wonder still, man learns their song, and soon it shall swell to the skies a mighty melody, the harmony of all earth's thousand tongues.

We need not leave our homes to seek by starlight some far-off shrine, for the Babe is no longer Bethlehem's pride and Mary's joy, but the whole wide world's, and the blessed burden of every heart that makes Him room.

Here we dedicate our rediscovered treasures, gold of royal love, frankincense of holy intercession, myrrh of healing sympathy, and bear them forth to bless all birth, and to make at every cradle a carol of welcome and a solemn service of the Christ. Amen.

THE ALTAR OF INCENSE

*Golden bowls, full of incense, which
are the prayers of the saints.*

—*Revelations* 5:8

ETERNAL, Holy, Almighty, whose name is Love; we are met in solemn company to seek Thy face, and in spirit and truth to worship Thy name. We come in deep humility, since Thou are so high and exalted, and because Thou beholdest the proud afar off. We come in tender penitence, for the contrite heart is Thy only dwelling. We come in the name and spirit of Jesus to make our wills one with Thine; to abandon our lonely and selfish walk for solemn communion with Thee, to put an end to sin by welcoming to our hearts Thy Holy Presence. Deeper than we have known, enter, Thou Maker of our souls; clearer than we have ever seen, dawn Thy glory on our sight. Light the flame upon the altar, call forth the incense of prayer, waken the song of praise, and manifest Thyself to all. Amen.

78 ৯৯

O SPIRIT of the Living God, breathe upon this assembled company Thy gracious power. Come to us as long ago upon the deep. Disturb our sleep, our pride, our apathy, and may those of us who have never before been conscious of our need, suddenly find ourselves hungering for Thee. Come upon us like a flame of fire. Cleanse us from moral pollution and from mental darkness. Search deep within, that to the core of self we may be clean.

Come to us as Thou camest to Jesus, constraining as a mother's love, giving us a new gentleness and grace, making us long for fellowship with all mankind, willing to bear the sins of the race.

Come to us as a rushing mighty wind, scattering the mists of our doubt, stirring our spirits to health and action, sweeping aside the fears that have held us in captivity.

Come, Holy Spirit, Come.

Amen.

O GOD, at whose commanding word light first sprang from darkness, we pray for the spreading of that light till the day break and the shadows flee away.

Send light unto our inmost souls, we pray, lest some cherished iniquity shut Thine ears to our prayers. Let the sunshine of Thy love stir our sterile natures into fruitfulness, and win from our stubborn soil a plenteous harvest of heavenly grain. Illumine the unknown tracts of our natures, that hidden powers may come to light and yield their service to Thy kingdom.

Shed light upon the dark places of the earth that the habitations of violence may be destroyed: let human misery melt away before the rising of the Sun of Righteousness.

Grant light upon the problems that perplex the mind of man, dispel the night of doubt and fear, and for the eyes that wait may morning dawn. Amen.

80 ⧟❧

O GOD of all wisdom, who knowest our needs before we ask, and art more ready to give than we are to recieve; pardon our pitiful worship and the peevishness of our prayers. We have nothing we can offer Thee except ourselves, and that is less than nothing. Yet because Thou didst make us and dost love us we yield ourselves to Thee, as we are, with all our struggles, our failures and our aspirations.

We have so often prayed for things that afterward we found would do us harm. We have asked Thee to save us from the pain and penalty of our sin; but now we feel there is nothing for us to do but leave ourselves in Thy hands, and no safe prayer for such as we but that Thy will be done.

We have sometimes wished we might become righteous in a moment, our sanctification suddenly accomplished; that our desires could be fulfilled without this weary wrestling of our will. Yet now we know the hunger after righteousness, the upward toil, the way of prayer and penitence is the only way, safe for us, and sure to lead at last to Thee.

Sometimes we have prayed, Hide Thy face from our sins; but now, Set them in the light of Thy countenance, be unto them as a consuming fire. Amen.

O GOD, forgive the poverty, the pettiness, the childish folly of our prayers. Listen,
not to our words, but to the groanings that
cannot be uttered; hearken, not to our petitions, but to the crying of our need. So often
we pray for that which is already ours, neglected and unappropriated; so often for that
which never can be ours; so often for that
which we must win ourselves; and then labor
endlessly for that which can only come to us
in prayer.

How often we have prayed for the coming of
Thy kingdom, yet when it has sought to come
through us we have sometimes barred the way;
we have wanted it without in others, but not
in our own hearts. We feel it is we who stand
between man's need and Thee; between ourselves and what we might be; and we have
no trust in our own strength, or loyalty, or
courage.

O give us to love Thy will, and seek Thy
kingdom first of all. Sweep away our fears,
our compromise, our weakness, lest at last we
be found fighting against Thee. Amen.

82 ৈ৵

ETERNAL holy Love, God most high, we seek to worship Thee not only in words and outward form, but in the depths of our spirit and in truth. We have only one offering; it is our poor selves; we give Thee but Thine own. We know only one way to Thee: the way of Jesus, the attitude of sonship and of childlike trust.

The perplexities of our strange natures drive us to Thee. We cannot understand ourselves. Glorious gleams and darkest shadows chase across our hearts; conflicts rage there while we stand helpless aside; within is no rest, without is no hope. Unless Thou canst rest us, O our God, we are exiles of eternity, homeless in infinite space.

The path to Thee has been tortuous and steep, our prayers fashioned in agony and moistened with tears. Help us to see that the path as well as the goal is Thyself; the prayer Thine, as the answer is Thine. End our search by beginning Thine. Steal upon us like the grace of summer evenings, like the dew on parched ground, like warm winds from sunnier lands. Lift our eyes to the hills, touch our aspirations, rest our longings in Thyself; for Thou hast made us. Amen.

O GOD, whose Spirit searcheth all things, and whose love beareth all things, encourage us to draw near to Thee in sincerity and in truth. Save us from a worship of the lips while our hearts are far away. Save us from the useless labor of attempting to conceal ourselves from Thee who searchest the heart.

Enable us to lay aside all those cloaks and disguises which we wear in the light of day and here to bare ourselves, with all our weakness, disease and sin, naked to Thy sight.

Make us strong enough to bear the vision of the truth, and to have done with all falsehood, pretense, and hypocrisy, so that we may see things as they are, and fear no more.

Enable us to look upon the love which has borne with us and the heart that suffers for us. Help us to acknowledge our dependence on the purity that abides our uncleanness, the patience that forgives our faithlessness, the truth that forbears all our falsity and compromise. And may we have the grace of gratitude, and the desire to dedicate ourselves to Thee. Amen.

84 ã»

O LIGHT of the world, shine upon us, O Sun of our spirits, reveal to us Thy comfort and Thy glory. We have sought for the light that never fades, for the glory that is never dimmed, that our eyes might be gladdened and the path of life made bright; and ofttimes found but darkness. The things that men rejoice in, the world's fame and power and riches, bring no glory that endures. We have seen the morn that promised fair turn to desolate and weeping noon, the crimson of the sunset sky has faded to the chill of night, and the majestic glittering heavens strike cold upon our sight.

And so we come back to the things we have neglected, to the common tasks, the stern commands of conscience, the sacrifice of love. We take the path that once we turned from, and climb mount Calvary. Surely this dolorous way is the path of light: we see the glory of God in the face of the Man of Sorrows; the solemn shadow of His cross is better than the sun.

Here where Man has triumphed and Thy great heart, O Father, is opened, we gather in adoring wonder at Thy glory, and in deep contrition at our own cowardice, failure and loveless lives. Amen.

O THOU that hearest prayer, to Thee
shall all flesh come. Before ever our yearning
has broken into speech. Thou hearest us. No
secret sigh of discontent escapes Thy listening
ear. No silent resolve on higher things but is
granted the assistance of Thy grace. We come
to Thee who already knowest us altogether;
ourselves, our hearts, our minds, our lives, all
shall be our prayer. Like desert travelers we
have thirsted after Thee, and Thou knowest
that thirst is Thine own creating. O satisfy us
early with Thy mercy.

We would spread before Thee all the spiritual deadness of our nature, the careless content, the unheeding soul, the short-sighted
vision. Thou hast made all Thy glory to pass
before us. We heard the thunder, we felt the
fire, but Thy still small voice of calm we were
too deaf to hear. O quicken us by Thy coming,
breath of God.

We confess to Thee that which has seared
our conscience; hours of riotous rebellion
which have left their mark, habits of self-
indulgence whose power grows greater with
the years, selfish determination to make life
minister only to ourselves.

O come, great Deliverer. Make known to
us Thy great salvation. Plant within us the
cross of Thy dear Son. May its pain awaken
and save us all. Amen.

86 ঌ

GREAT Shepherd of Thy people, who knowest all, and callest us by that secret name which unlocks the heart to Thy presence, we are folded together and wait for Thy coming. Take us one by one and shut us in with Thyself. Light in every heart some overwhelming vision of Thyself. Draw us apart to be with Thee.

Ofttimes Thou hast called us, but our ears have been dulled with other cries; now make us deaf to every voice but Thine. We are each one living alone, despite our friendship and our common life. We have feared to walk in desert places, we have loved the garish day, we have been afraid to be left alone with ourselves, lest long-stifled voices should speak something we dreaded to hear. We have been afraid of Thee; afraid because we do not truly know Thee. Thou hast been to us as the darkness is to children, as the dread unknown to the fearful and untraveled soul.

Come to us through the silence, in the night, meet us in the desert, or, if we shun the lonely way, meet us in the crowd, reveal Thyself in the intercourse of life, speak above the tumult in thunder to our souls. Amen.

O THOU who art of purer eyes than to behold iniquity, canst Thou bear to look on us conscious of our great transgression? Yet hide not Thy face from us, for in Thy light alone shall we see light.

Forgive us for the sins which crowd into the mind as we realize Thy presence; our ungovernable tempers, our shuffling insincerities, the craven fear of our hearts, the pettiness of our spirits, the foul lusts and fatal leanings of our souls. Not for pardon only, but for cleansing, Lord, we pray.

Forgive us, we beseech Thee, our unconscious sins; things which must be awful to Thy sight, of which we yet know nothing. Forgive by giving us in fuller measure the awakening of Thy presence, that we may know ourselves, and lose all love of sin in the knowledge of what Thou art.

Forgive us for the things for which we can never forgive ourselves; those sad turned pages of our life which some chance wind of memory blows back again with shame; for the moment of cruel passion, the hour beyond recall, the word that went forth to poison and defame, the carelessness that lost our opportunity, the unheeded fading of bright ideals.

Forgive us for the things that others can never forgive; the idle tale, the cruel wrong, the uncharitable condemnation, the unfair judgment, the careless criticism, the irresponsible conduct.

Forgive us for the sins of our holy things; that we have turned the sacred page without a sigh, read the confessions of holy men and women and never joined therein, lived in Thy light and never prayed to be forgiven or rendered Thee thanksgiving; professed to believe in Thee and love Thee, yet dared to injure and hate.

Naught save being born again, nothing but a miracle of grace, can ever be to us forgiveness. Cleanse our hearts, renew our minds, and take not Thy Holy Spirit from us. Amen.

ETERNAL God, who hast formed us, and designed us for companionship with Thee; who hast called us to walk with Thee and be not afraid; forgive us, we pray Thee, if craven fear, unworthy thought, or hidden sin has prompted us to hide from Thee. Remove the suspicion which regards Thy service as an intrusion on our time and an interference with our daily task. Show to us the life that serves Thee in the quiet discharge of each day's duty, that ennobles all our toil by doing it as unto Thee. We ask for no far-off vision which shall set us dreaming while opportunities around slip by; for no enchantment which shall make our hands to slack and our spirits to sleep, but for the vision of Thyself in common things for every day; that we may find a Divine calling in the claims of life, and see a heavenly reward in work well done. We ask Thee not to lift us out of life, but to prove Thy power within it; not for tasks more suited to our strength, but for strength more suited to our tasks. Give to us the vision that moves, the strength that endures, the grace of Jesus Christ, who wore our flesh like a monarch's robe and walked out earthly life like a conqueror in triumph.

Amen.

89 ɞ

ETERNAL Father, most real when most invisible, most near when we think Thee far away, most clearly conceived when we acknowledge Thee to be incomprehensible; speak to us not only from the past, but from the living present, not only from the awful silences, but in every tumultuous thought, not only from the clouds that veil Thy heavenly throne, but from Thine image graven on the heart of man.

While our thoughts of Thee grow wider, may we remember how vaster still Thou art, and may we seek to grow more sensible of Thy presence and to reflect Thee more purely in our lives.

Help us, O King of Ages, in these changing times and these troubled days. Lose not care of us when we lose sight of Thee. Still hold us fast when faith is feeble and knowledge is confused. If our thoughts of Thee should grow doubtful and Thine image within be dimmed, may we unconsciously fulfill Thy will. Help us to remember that it is not to him that thinketh, but to him that doeth, that Thy will is known. Help us to believe that Thou abidest beyond all change, and art always better than our highest hopes, greater than our noblest thoughts. Amen.

MOST Holy Father, we thank Thee for the inner kingdom of the mind, for the glories which eye hath not seen nor ear heard. We thank Thee for Thy footprints in creation and for Thy glory in the face of man. Save us, we pray, from all sins of intellect; not only from the error and ignorance which belong to our frailty, but from prejudice and all un-reason, from mental insincerity, from lack of rational control, and from blasphemy against the Holy Spirit. Help us through sincerity, singlemindedness, and enthusiasm to enter the kingdom that is open to all believers.

Give us, above all, grace and endurance to plant Thy kingdom in the world in which we live, by love of truth, by striving after justice, by following fearless wherever light may lead, and by giving ourselves, if needs be, even unto death. Amen.

91 ॐ

O IMMANUEL, God for ever with us, help us to make a place for Thee to reign within our hearts, to build in these our days that city where Thou shalt dwell with men, and sin and darkness, pain and sorrow, shall be no more.

We thank Thee that Christ cometh to us ever more manifest and more victorious. We pray that this age may become as the highway of our God; may the desires that stir among the people exalt every valley and make every mountain low.

When we grow contented with the things that are, send us again the prophet's word. When we soil our souls with sin, open then in our midst the cleansing fountain. When in our selfishness we sell men into bondage and humble our women with shame, come again from the ranks of those who toil; from the lands that are in darkness, from our despised Nazareths, raise up the Deliverer. When we grow proud of our petty knowledge, and can no longer stoop to learn Thy ways, send us a child again, a new generation springing from the uncorrupted source of things, and lead us back to a sane mind, a sincere heart, and a simple life.

Though poor be the chamber, shrink not from its lowliness; abhor not the womb of our humanity; be born again in us, assume our flesh and lift us to Thyself. Amen.

O LORD, may we not imagine, because the world is old and worn, that all things shall continue as they are, and we can comfort our hearts and take our ease. We cannot tell at what moment hidden fires may flame forth and consume the habitations we have builded for our souls. May we not be found wanting at the testing time; all we have labored for prove like stubble to the flame; the foundations we have chosen, only sinking sand.

Though the days drift dreaming by, may we not conclude they count for naught. Help us to remember that the book of life is being written, the account is being rendered, the harvest is ripening, the sickle is thrust in, the axe is at the root of the tree, the judge is at the gate. May we be counted worthy to stand before the Son of Man, and to abide His coming who is like a refiner's fire.

We see the long content of the peoples breaking down. We hear voices that challenge all that men have counted final, fixed and sure; the foundations of things are shaken, men's hearts are failing them for fear. Enable us to lift up our heads because our redemption draweth nigh, to trim our lamps, and at the midnight cry go forth to meet the Bridegroom.

Amen.

93 ৯৯

O THOU, the Hope of Israel, the Saviour thereof in time of trouble, why shouldest Thou be as a sojourner with us, as a wayfaring man who turneth aside to tarry for a night? Thou art in the midst of us; leave us not. Thou who hast set the hope of Thy revelation in the hearts of all, manifest Thyself to us. Thou who hast spoken in times past by the prophets and in the fullness of time hast revealed Thyself in one who was a Son, enable us to realize that Thou abidest with us always. Dwell with us in glorious splendor, enthrone Thyself among the nations, walk in our midst, and be to us Immanuel. Amen.

GREAT Father, we thank Thee that we have not to wait for Thine advent, for all history is Thy coming, and Thou are here. From the hour when Thy Spirit stirred the dark primeval deep till Jesus by the bench and on the mountain top cried, "Abba Father," our world has been growing more conscious of Thy presence. And yet we wait for something more; strange hopes stir the hearts of men and passionate prayers break forth from their lips. Can it be that this further revelation waits upon our faith and rests with our endeavor?

We have grown unconscious of our need, become accustomed to things remaining as they are; ceased to desire things different, lost our vision and are ready to perish. Worst of all, we have found ourselves unwilling to pay the price of better things. We have desired Thy coming, but not through us, we have sought a salvation that would leave ourselves still unchanged; we have prayed that Thy will might be done, but we have shrunk from doing it first and alone.

Stand Thou before us like the light, like love all lovely, like the morning. Then surely we shall hinder Thee no more. Amen.

95 ॐ

O GOD, for whose advent Thy weary world has waited long, save us lest in these latter days the hope of Thee grow dim, and we, forgetting to watch with lamps trimmed and loins girded, find ourselves unprepared to meet Thee, when at midnight comes the cry.

For we know our hopes cannot lie. In the past we can discern that Thou hast surely come; in the prophets and in the Word made flesh; in the downfall of empires, and the rising of the peoples; in the strange thoughts that stir the world, in the dawning sense of brotherhood. But not yet dost Thou wholly dwell amongst us.

We mourn the misunderstandings and suspicions that arm the nations, the growing alienation and strife between class and class, our failure to find a common faith or a religion to unite us all. Come and heal our divisions, and enable us to find that one highway along which we may march together to the Promised Land.

Grant that we may be found with those prophets and forerunners who, knowing the mind of God and the times of His restoration, prepared the way of the Lord.

Forbid that when Thou comest Thou shouldest not find faith upon the earth. Amen.

MOST merciful Father, strengthen our faith we beseech Thee, lest we fail to endure to the end, and miss Thy great salvation. The days hang heavy on our hands, the evening often finds the morning promise unfulfilled, and hope deferred makes sick the heart. Sometimes we fear we cannot hold out much longer.

O God, make haste to help us.

We have hailed with high enthusiasm some mighty movement which should set the peoples free, only to see the battle go against the righteous cause, to find its principles betrayed for a handful of silver, its lofty dreams dispersed before the cold unyielding facts of life. And still the faces of the poor are ground, men labor for naught, and one slavery rises from the ruins of another.

When wilt Thou save the people?

We have striven to follow Jesus Christ, we have tried to forgive our enemies, we have humbled ourselves before haughty and cruel men; but we have not changed their hearts. Kindness has been met by cruelty, confidence by betrayal, trust by mean advantage, hopes by disappointment. We are tempted to despair of Christ's slow and patient ways.

Let not our hearts harden into stone.

We have gathered with those who love the Name of Jesus, we have sought the communion of saints, the fellowship of the Church, only to find the world entrenched therein; men earnestly contending for the faith they do not believe, praying prayers they hope will never be answered. Help us through good report and ill to seek the purity of Thy Church, the unity of the body of Christ.

O for the patience of Jesus Christ.

Amen.

97 ૐ

MERCIFUL Father, to whom all sons of men are dear, we pray for all that sit in darkness and in the shadow of death, that the Dayspring from on high may visit them; for the poor and oppressed, for those who dwell amid ugliness and squalor, far from loveliness and purity, and for whom the fire-gemmed heavens shine in vain; for those who toil beyond their strength and beyond Thine ordinance, without pleasure in the work of their hands, and without help of rest; for those who sink back to the beast and seek to drown all thought and feeling, and for all who are trampled under foot by men. Raise up deliverance for the peoples.

For those who in their plenty live delicately, contemn the poor, and forget God; for all people whose hearts are so perished within them that pity has departed. Show them Thy ways. Amen.

O GOD, who hast made of one blood
all the nations of mankind, so that all are
children and members one of another, how
is it that we are so slow to trace the family
likeness, so reluctant to claim our common
kinship? We pray Thee, O our God, to make
the peoples one.

We pray for the Church of Christ so broken,
scattered and dismembered, that none would
think we followed all one Lord and held a
common faith. Purge away the vanity, intoler-
ance, and unforgiving spirit which keep us far
apart. May the seamless robe not be utterly
rent, nor the body any longer broken.

We pray that since man's need is one, we
all may find the one way to Thee, the one
God. Forbid that in our highest things we
should find fellowship impossible. May the
spirit of Christ break down all barriers and
answer the desire of all nations.

We pray for a union so deep and universal
that it shall gather all within one fold: those
who pray and those who cannot; those whose
faith is firm, and those whose doubt is slow
to clear. May we never be content with aught
that excludes another from the fullness of
Thy grace, a single soul from the welcome of
Thy heart. Amen.

99 ﴾

O GOD, the Light of such as seek Thee, grant to our minds that illumination without which we walk in darkness and know not whither we go. Our hearts, like orphaned children, cry out for Thee, Thou only companion of man's soul. May we feel Thy presence about us and be allowed to love Thee, sinful though we be. Condescend to walk with us in the devious ways of life, granting us on earth the friendship of Heaven, shepherding us in danger, piloting us through the storm.

Remember all such as feel no need of Thee, who seem content with a careless, unexamined life, whose hearts are unvisited by desires of better things. Leave them not to themselves, lest they go down to death and destruction, but startle them with Thy call, awaken them with Thy light, brood upon their spirits until they stir to greet Thee.

Be especially gracious to all prodigal souls who would turn to Thee if they only dared, but fear for the greatness of their sin, the despite done to Thy grace, the long delay of their repentance. Make known the tenderness of Thy compassion, reveal the grief of Thy heart, disclose the long-suffering of Thy love, that they may rise and come to Thee. Amen.

O GOD, who hatest nothing that Thou hast made, carest for Thy creation more than men care for their property, and lovest every soul of man more than a mother her only child; may this same care and love displace man's inhumanity and selfishness, until, in a new sense of the beauty of man's body and the eternal value of his soul, cruelty and neglect, pain and sorrow pass away.

We pray for the coming of the commonwealth where those who toil shall be honored and rewarded, where a man's worth shall be reckoned higher than the price of the things he fashions with hand or brain, where science shall serve, not destruction or private gain, but preservation and the common good.

We remember those who labor continually under the danger of death, that others may be protected, warmed, and comforted. We are conscious of the sacrifice that others are called upon to make on our behalf. We remember those who are ready to lay down their lives for the preservation of our peace and the provision of our needs. May we so live that such sacrifice shall not have been in vain. May the whole community be stirred to wonder whether men need suffer as they do.

Give inspiration to those who labor at the perfecting of protective science, and who seek the redemption of the workers. Make a new tie of blood sacrifice between us all. Since Thou didst, to our confusion and amazement, declare Thy nature most of all in the Craftsman of Nazareth, so once again may redemption spring from the ranks of those who toil.

We do not ask to pass beyond the things of sense and time, but to see in them Thy presence; in the crises of our times, Thy judgments; in the rising demand for righteousness, the coming of Thy kingdom. Amen.

THE HOLY PLACE

Let us draw near with a true heart, in full assurance of faith.

—*Hebrews 10:22*

ALMIGHTY God, seeing that it is high time to awake out of sleep, since the night is far spent and the day is at hand: help us to put off the works of darkness and put on the armor of light.

May our loins be girt and our lamps burning, and ourselves as men who watch for the coming of their Lord. Amen.

O GOD, who art to be found by those who truly seek Thee, known by those who love, seen by those whose heart is pure; Thy Spirit possesses all things, speaks in the holy dawn, calls in the quiet even, broods on the deep, and dwells in the heart of man.

Forgive us if we, made to commune with Thee, whose lives were ordered to walk with Thee, have grown insensible to Thy presence, have rested in the things that appear, grown careless of the eternal and the holy. Send now some word of Thine to make a highway to our hearts, and Thyself draw near. Shut us in gathered here, in with Thyself, alone, until every heart burns and each spirit moves toward Thee. May the Spirit of Jesus come upon us and make us at home with Thee.
Amen.

103 ৵

O THOU who transcendest all thought of Thee as the heavens are higher than the earth; we acknowledge that we cannot search Thee out to perfection, but we thank Thee that Thou, the Invisible, comest to us in the things that are seen; that Thy exceeding glory is shadowed in the flower that blooms for a day, in the light that fades; that Thine infinite love has been incarnate in lowly human life; and that Thy presence surrounds all our ignorance. Thy holiness our sin, Thy peace our unrest.

Give us that lowly heart which is the only temple that can contain the infinite. Save us from the presumption that prides itself on a knowledge which is not ours, and from the hypocrisy and carelessness which professes an ignorance which Thy manifestation has made for ever impossible. Save us from calling ourselves by a name that Thou alone canst wear, and from despising the image of Thyself Thou hast formed us to bear, and grant that knowledge of Thee revealed in Jesus Christ which is our eternal life. Amen.

104 ॐ

BREATHE on us, breath of God; not as the mighty rushing wind, lest the dimly burning flax be quenched; but with the quiet breath that shall fan to flame our smoldering faith. Inward Presence of our God, we cannot do without Thee! Unless first we hear the gentle whisper of Thy voice, the majesty of fire and story, the glories of earth and heaven, will pass in meaningless pageantry before us. The sacred page of the past and the slowly traced bible of today will alike be closed to us. As we address ourselves to seek our God, light Thou our hearts with His presence. As we turn to think of Jesus, make our hearts to burn with love. Spirit of the Living God, Spirit of Jesus, Spirit who choosest man's mind for Thy dwelling; make Thyself known to us now.

Amen.

105 ৡৈ

MOST Holy Father may the hush of Thy presence move us now to adoration, and may all voices be stilled that Thine may be heard. Quiet our minds of their fretting, hide from us the false glamor of things, and may the truth dawn upon all our souls. We bring to Thee the unsatisfied desire of our seeking hearts, for naught save Thyself can give us rest.

Show to us the great secret of Thyself, give us some image of Thee in our thought that we may know who and what Thou art. We want to stand before the awful purity of Thy throne, yea, even though it destroy us; we would see Thy face though we may never after see aught else. We want to know the measure of Thy love, even though it break our hearts. We want to see the hidden purposes of Thy will, even though the vision change our little plans and flood our lives beyond our power to hold.

We want not only to see Thee thus in the mystic hour of revelation, but in broadening purposes in the history of our time; not only in the Shekinah of the Holy Place, but at work in our common days, inhabiting our narrow hearts.

Incarnate Thyself, O Invisible, that these eyes may be for ever satisfied; may Thy word become flesh and the unutterable take voice. O come, O come, Immanuel. Amen.

LOVE Divine, Love lowly hearted, our city's gates stand widely open to Thy welcome. Without Thee the people is uncrowned, tumult and rebellion break forth, truth is perished in the streets, and justice fallen at our gates. Come and establish Thy kingdom in our midst, sending peace on the earth, peace in the hearts of men.

Apart from Thee all temples stand desolate, unblessed by sacrifice, unsanctified by altar fires, unhallowed by thankful song. Though they have been desecrated by unholy traffic, polluted by sin, deserted for an easier worship of the world, come Thou, and by Thy presence cleanse, inhabit, and restore.

God unimaginable. God most near, God of the tender Jesus, God of His bitter cross; hear us, Thy little ones, as we cry "HOSANNA in the highest; blessed is He that cometh in the name of the Lord." Lift up your heads, O ye gates, and be ye lifted up ye everlasting doors, and the King of glory shall come in. Amen.

107 ᓚ

LIKE summer seas that lave with silent tides a lonely shore, like whispering winds that stir the tops of forest trees, like a still small voice that calls us in the watches of the night, like a child's hand that feels about a fast-closed door; gentle, unnoticed, and oft in vain; so is Thy coming unto us, O God.

Like ships storm-driven into port, like starving souls that seek the bread they once despised, like wanderers begging refuge from the whelming night, like prodigals that seek the father's home when all is spent; yet welcomed at the open door, arms outstretched and kisses for our shame; so is our coming unto Thee, O God.

Like flowers uplifted to the sun, like trees that bend before the storm, like sleeping seas that mirror cloudless skies, like a harp to the hand, like an echo to a cry, like a song to the heart; for all our stubbornness, our failure and our sin; so would we have been to Thee, O God. Amen.

ETERNAL God, before whose eyes the ages pass, who knowest all the changing thoughts of man; help us to remember that Thou art throned above all time and bringest every thought into captivity unto Thyself.

May we not turn back to bygone centuries to hear Thy voice, as if Thou spakest no longer to us now. May we not imagine that the judgment is postponed to some far-off future day. Give us to know that upon the slopes of Sinai still our feet may stand, and even now the books are opened, and the thrones are set.

Enable us to remember that all souls are Thine, that their innermost secrets are naked and open to Thee, and that none can ever fall beyond Thy reach or wander outside Thy concern.

So help us all in this hour to realize the presence of eternity that we trifle not our time away; the nearness of Thine awful judgment, lest we forget what manner of men we are; the long-suffering of Thy love, lest at thought of Thee we grow afraid. Amen.

109 ବକ

O GOD, who so fillest all things that they only thinly veil Thy presence; we adore Thee in the beauty of the world, in the goodness of human hearts and in Thy thought within the mind. We praise Thee for the channels through which Thy grace can come to us; sickness and health, joy and pain, freedom and necessity, sunshine and rain, life and death.

We thank Thee for all the gentle and healing ministries of life; the gladness of the morning, the freedom of the wind, the music of the rain, the joy of the sunshine and the deep calm of the night; for trees, and flowers, and clouds, and skies; for the tender ministries of human love, the unselfishness of parents, the love that binds man and woman, the confidence of little children; for the patience of teachers and the encouragement of friends.

We bless Thee for the stirring ministry of the past, for the story of noble deeds, the memory of holy men, the printed book, the painter's art, the poet's craft; most of all for the ministry of the Son of Man who taught us the eternal beauty of earthly things, who by His life set us free from fear, and by His death won us from our sins to Thee; for His cradle, His cross, and His crown.

May His Spirit live within us, conquer all the selfishness of man, and take away the sin of the world. Amen.

WE praise Thee, O our Father, for this world and its witness of Thee: for sunshine, wind and rain, and all weathers; for the wide-bosomed sea and the everlasting hills; for high sailing clouds and clear shining stars; for springing grass and flowers and tall stately trees; for lakes and streams and all waters. Help us to drink to the full of the beauty and strength of the world and to know that they come from Thee as gifts of love to us.

We praise Thee for man and for his making in Thine image: for the strange light in his eyes, for his wonderful face, his mighty mind and his deathless soul; for his lordship of creation, his power to conquer nature, his skill to plant and build, to fashion and create, to paint and sing; for the memories of greatness that abide his fall, for the grace of forgiveness that restores his soul, for the cords of love that bind him to Thy will. Hasten the day of redemption, when our last enemy shall be trodden under foot and Thou shalt call the son of man to share Thine everlasting throne.

We praise Thee for the sacrament of Life: for its great adventure, its glorious opportunities, its zeal, its triumph, its desire; for the things that point beyond themselves to a spiritual realm from which they take their rise; for the failures that quicken better hopes, the pains and sorrows and sins that spur us on to search for health and comfort and redemption; for death that wakens thoughts of eternal life, for unfulfilled desire that anchors us to Thee; for all ministries of the infinite: the beauty of common things, the light of heaven upon our daily path, Thy glory in the face of Jesus Christ and the Holy Spirit's witness in the soul of man.

Now we know that all things are through and for and unto Christ, and in Him all things are ours. Heaven and earth are full of Thy glory. Glory be to Thee, O Lord most High.

Amen.

O GOD above all, yet in all; holy beyond all imagination, yet friend of sinners;
who inhabitest the realms of unfading light,
yet leadest us through the shadows of mortal
life; how solemn and uplifting it is even to
think upon Thee. Like sight of sea to wearied
eyes, like a walled-in garden to the troubled
mind, like home to wanderer, like a strong
tower to a soul pursued; so to us is the sound
of Thy name.

But greater still to feel Thee in our heart;
like a river glorious, cleansing, healing, bringing life; like a song victorious, comforting our
sadness, banishing our care; like a voice calling us to battle, urging us beyond ourselves.

But greater far to know Thee as our Father,
as dear as Thou art near; and ourselves be-
gotten of Thy love, made in Thy image, cared
for through all our days, never beyond Thy
sight, never out of Thy thought.

To think of Thee is rest; to know Thee is
eternal life; to see Thee is the end of all desire;
to serve Thee is perfect freedom and everlasting joy. Amen.

112 ও৵

O GOD, we thank Thee for the world in which Thou hast placed us, for the universe whose vastness is revealed in the blue depths of the sky, whose immensities are lit by shining stars beyond the strength of mind to follow. We thank Thee for every sacrament of beauty; for the sweetness of flowers, the solemnity of the stars, the sound of streams and swelling seas; for far-stretching lands and mighty mountains which rest and satisfy the soul, the purity of dawn which calls to holy dedication, the peace of evening which speaks of everlasting rest. May we not fear to make this world for a little while our home, since it is Thy creation and we ourselves are part of it. Help us humbly to learn its laws and trust its mighty powers.

We thank Thee for the world within, deeper than we dare to look, higher than we care to climb; for the great kingdom of the mind and the silent spaces of the soul. Help us not to be afraid of ourselves, since we were made in Thy image, loved by Thee before the worlds began, and fashioned for Thy eternal habitation. May we be brave enough to bear the truth, strong enough to live in the light, glad to yield ourselves to Thee.

We thank Thee for that world brighter and better than all, opened for us in the broken heart of the Saviour; for the universe of love and purity in Him, for the golden sunshine of His smile, the tender grace of His forgiveness, the red renewing rain and crimson flood of His great sacrifice. May we not shrink from its searching and surpassing glory, nor, when this world fades away, fear to commit ourselves to that world which shall be our everlasting home. Amen.

113 ॐ

O THOU who hast visited us with the Dayspring from on high, who hast made light to shine in the darkness, we praise Thy holy name and proclaim Thy wonderful goodness.

We bless Thee for the dawning of the light in far-off ages so soon as human eyes could bear its rays. We remember those who bore aloft the torch of truth when all was false and full of shame; those far-sighted souls who from the mountain tops of vision heralded the coming day; those who labored in the darkened valleys to lift men's eyes to the hills.

We thank Thee that in the fullness of the times Thou didst gather Thy light into life, so that even simple folk could see; for Jesus the Star of the morning and the Light of the world.

We commemorate His holy nativity, His lowly toil, His lonely way; the gracious words of His lips, the deep compassion of His heart, His friendship for the fallen, His love for the outcast; the crown of thorns, the cruel cross, the open shame. And we rejoice to know as He was here on earth, so Thou art eternally. Thou dost not abhor our flesh, nor shrink from our earthly toil. Thou rememberest our frailty, bearest with our sin, and tastest even our bitter cup of death.

And now we rejoice for the light that shines about our daily path from the cradle to the grave, and for the light that illumines its circuit beyond these spheres from our conception in Thy mind to the day when we wake in Thy image; for the breathing of Thy spirit into ours till we see Thee face to face: in God; from God; to God at last.

Hallelujah.

Amen.

114 ҉

O THOU that turnest the shadow of death into the morning, on this day of days our hearts exult with heavenly joy. All things conspire to make us sure of Thee: the gracious sunshine, the stir of springtime, the morning rapture of the birds; but greater far, a secret thrill runs through the air from far-off days.

Easter day breaks! Christ rises! Mercy every way is infinite.

The clouds are vanished from the sky, doubts are driven from the mind, Thou hast conquered our last enemy, and our tongues are filled with singing. Pain has been our portion here, but now we know that in all pain there lies the promise of redemption. Thou dost plan our lives to cross the valley of Humiliation, to climb the hill Difficulty, and then at last descend where waits the shadow feared by man. But now we know it is a shadow only. The grim-barred gates of death swing back, and the glory from an endless world shine through, beyond the mind's imagining, beyond our hearts' desire. Our Jesus now is crowned with glory, clothed in victory, and vested with the keys of death and hell.

Praise be unto Thee, O Lord most high.

Amen.

FATHER of life, and God of the living, Fountain of our being and Light of all our day; we thank Thee for that knowledge of Thyself which lights our life with eternal splendor, for that giving of Thyself which has made us partakers of Thy divine nature. We bless Thee for everything around us which ministers Thee to our minds; for the greatness and glory of nature, for the history of our race, and the lives of noble men; for the thoughts of Thee expressed in human words, in the art of painters and musicians, in the work of builders and craftsmen. We bless Thee for the constant memories of what we are that rise within ourselves; for the pressure of duty, the hush of solemn thoughts, for moments of insight when the veil on the face of all things falls away, for hours of high resolve when life is quickened within, for seasons of communion when, earth and sense forgotten, heaven holds our silent spirits raptured and aflame.

We have learned to praise Thee for the darker days when we had to walk by faith, for weary hours that strengthened patience and endeavor, for moments of gloom and times of depression which taught us to trust, not to changing tides of feeling, but to Thee who changest not. And now since Christ has won His throne by His cross of shame, risen from His tomb to reign for ever in the hearts of men, we know that nothing can ever separate us from Thee; that in all conflicts we may be more than conquerors; that all dark and hostile things shall be transformed and work for good to those who know the secret of Thy love.

Glory be to Thee, O Lord.

Amen.

116 ह

O GOD, there are sounds on the earth and signs in the heaven that quicken all hearts with expectation: nations that long have sat in darkness and the shadow of death, turning to the light; peoples that long have worn the yoke of tyranny rising to shake themselves free; murmurs of the masses too long content with slavery; thoughts that threaten the order of all things and predict the shaking of the foundations of the world. We listen to hear if these are the sounds of Thy chariot wheels; we lift our heads to see if the dawn is reddening in the sky.

We dare to watch for Thy fuller coming to us. For the complete manifestation of Thyself, for the emancipation of humanity from fear, sin, doubt and despair.

We dare to pray that Thou shouldest make Thy entrance through our hearts. Even so, Lord Jesus; come quickly. Amen.

ETERNAL and Gracious Father, whose presence comforteth like sunshine after rain; we thank Thee for Thyself and for all Thy revelation to us. Our hearts are burdened with thanksgiving at the thought of all Thy mercies; for all the blessings of this mortal life, for health, for reason, for learning and for love; but far beyond all thought and thankfulness, for Thy great redemption. It was no painless travail that brought us to the birth, it has been no common patience that has borne with us all this while; long-suffering love, and the breaking of the eternal heart alone could reconcile us to the life to which Thou hast ordained us. We have seen the Son of Man sharing our sickness and shrinking not from our shame, we have beheld the Lamb of God bearing the sins of the world, we have mourned at the mysterious passion and stood astonished at the cross of Jesus Christ; and behind all we have had the vision of an altar-throne and one thereon slain from the foundation of the world; heard a voice calling us that was full of tears; seen beyond the veil that was rent, the agony of God.

O for a thousand tongues to sing the love that has redeemed us. O for a thousand lives that we might yield them all to Thee. Amen.

118 ह&

O FATHER of mankind, whose mind embraces our multitudinous humanity, whose heart is wide to harbor all our race, who knowest all as a shepherd knows his sheep; let the knowledge of Thyself enter every mind, bringing freedom, forgiveness and faith to all the sons of men.

Though the ages stretch beyond our grasp and burden our imagination, Thou holdest them all in Thy mind as a moment. Though the worlds are scattered like dust through endless space, Thou bringest out their host by number and callest them all by name. Though life puts forth her myriad forms and wastes herself on vain designs, Thou holdest all in the hollow of Thy hand, so that not one falls forgotten or perishes purposeless in pain. Though the march of man reaches from the dust to the dawn, from the slime to the soul, from the abyss to the throne, and though the generations rise and pass away, Thou leadest everyone; from the womb to the tomb, from the mother's breast to the breast of God; guiding little feet, guarding youth's glad steps, giving strength to the weary, and gathering all souls to Thyself at the last.

Though we wrest ourselves from Thy will, lose ourselves in our selfishness, run riot in rebellion, and make sin our shame; though we make seven hells for our souls, Thou still dost hold us and canst draw us back to Thee.

Therefore we bless Thee that Thou didst give us being; praise Thee Thou didst form us of Thy substance; thank Thee Thou dost destine us to know Thy love, share Thy name, and live for evermore in the blessedness of Thy being and the glory of Thy Godhead.

Amen.

119 ঽ✏

O FATHER Eternal, we thank Thee for the new and living way into Thy presence made for us in Christ; the way of trust, sincerity and sacrifice. Beneath His cross we would take our stand, in communion with His Spirit would we pray, in fellowship with the whole Church of Christ we would seek to know Thy mind and will.

We desire to know all the fullness of Christ, to appropriate His unsearchable riches, to feed on His humanity whereby Thou hast become to us the bread of our inmost souls and the wine of life, to become partakers of Thy nature, share Thy glory and become one with Thee through Him.

Give unto us fellowship with His sufferings and insight into the mystery of His cross, so that we may be indeed crucified with Him, be raised to newness of life, and be hidden with Christ in Thee.

We desire to make thankful offering of ourselves as members of the body of Christ; in union with all the members may we obey our unseen Head, so that the Body may be undivided, and Thy love, and healing power, and very Self may be incarnate on the earth in one Holy Universal Church. Amen.

ETERNAL God, who art above all change and darkness, whose will begat us, and whose all present love doth enfold and continually redeem us, Holy Guest who indwellest, and dost comfort us; we have gathered to worship Thee, and in communion with Thee to find ourselves raised to the Light of our life, and the Heaven of our desires.

Pour upon our consciousness the sense of Thy wonderful nearness to us. Reveal to our weakness and distress the power and the grace that are more than sufficient for us. May we see what we are, Thy Spirit-born children linked by nature, love and choice to Thy mighty being; and may the vision make all fears to fade, and a Divine strength to pulse within.

Enable us to carry out from this place the peace and strength that here we gain, to take into our homes a kinder spirit, a new thoughtfulness; that we may brighten sadness, heal the sick, and make happiness to abound. May we take into our daily tasks and life of labor, a sense of righteousness that shall be as salt to every evil and corrupting influence.

Because we have walked here awhile with Thee, may we be able to walk more patiently with man. Send us forth with love to the fallen, hope for the despairing, strength to impart to the weak and wayward; and carry on through us the work Thou didst commence in Thy Son our Brother Man and Saviour God. Amen.

The Lord bless and keep thee:
The Lord make His face to shine
  upon thee:
The Lord lift up His countenance
  upon thee, and give thee peace.

—*Numbers 6:24-26*